how to

Make Decisions
About People

Charles A. Dailey
Frederick C. Dyer

how to

Make Decisions
About People

parker publishing company, inc.

WEST NYACK,
NEW YORK

PRINTED IN THE UNITED STATES OF AMERICA
42104—B&P

About the Authors

CHARLES A. DAILEY

In 1964, Dr. Charles A. Dailey became Director of the Industrial Relations - Personnel Program in the School of Business Administration, The American University. Before that (1957-1964), he headed the executive development program at Interstate Bakeries Corporation—an organization operating 34 plants and doing over $160 millions worth of sales a year.

In 1950, Dr. Dailey was awarded a Doctor of Philosophy degree in Psychology by the University of Michigan. He has had experience as a naval officer (in World War II), as a hospital psychologist, as an industrial psychologist, and as a management consultant. In 1961, he formed the RADET Company (RADET stands for *Research And Development in Education and Training*), which he still heads. This company develops programmed courses (teaching machine approaches) for training in human relations and in decision-making about people. The RADET Company has published his two short books (*The Study of Lives*, with Robert Wright, 1963; and *A Programmed Case Course*, 1964).

In his specialty of leadership selection and development he has made major speeches before such audiences as the national convention of the American Society of Training Directors, the International Congress of Psychology, the

Industrial College of the Armed Forces, the Church Executive Development Program, and the Air Capital Management Conference. He has published articles in the *Journal of Psychology, Human Relations, Psychological Reports, Journal of Clinical Psychology,* and similar professional journals. He is a member of the American Association for the Advancement of Science and the American Psychological Association. Because of his work, Dr. Dailey is listed in *American Men of Science* and in *Leaders in American Science.*

Among the clients he advises as a consultant are a research and development aerospace company, a supermarket chain, a firm of CPA's, and a variety of other organizations.

FREDERICK C. DYER

Frederick C. Dyer, Special Assistant to the Under Secretary of the Navy for Civilian Management Training and Executive Development, has had experience in aircraft manufacturing and in the insurance business, as well as in military and government service. He has his A.B. from Holy Cross College and his M.B.A. from Dartmouth College. He has served as a professorial lecturer or adjunct professor in the graduate courses in management at The George Washington University and the Drexel Institute of Technology. He has written over a dozen books for the U.S. Government, and their total copies in print number over 3 million. His eight commercially published books have totalled ten book club selections, and one of them has been translated into Spanish. He has written articles for most of the major management magazines and has been a speaker before many groups in various parts of the country. In 1961 the Navy gave him its Superior Civilian Service Award, and in 1963 the Governor of Nebraska appointed him an Admiral in the Nebraska State Navy. He is a member of the American Association for the Advancement of Science, the Authors League, the Society for the Advancement of Management, and the Society of Technical Writers and Editors.

Acknowledgements

Making the following acknowledgements is more than a duty; it is a pleasant way of evoking memories of colleagues, mentors, and supporters.

Charles Dailey wishes to remember in particular: Nathan Baily, Robert Corrigan, Roy Doty, John Dow, Robert English, S.P. English, Ernest Hueter, Max Hutt, Edward Lucking, Robert Piltz, Clarke Thornton, Ben Tregoe, Dan Uhrig, John Van de Water, Robert Wald, Harry Woodward, and Robert Wright.

Similarly, Fred Dyer acknowledges all that he learned from and all the kindnesses he received from: David Bagley, Kenneth BeLieu, Ray Crosby, John Cocci, Paul Fay, Tom Hardy, W. P. Mack, W. J. Saylor, Thornton Moore, John V. Noel, Ed Pace, Charles Peck, E. D. Schmitz, J. V. Smith, W. T. Sutherland, Boone D. Tillett, George Thomas, Ed Wiggenhorn, and E. R. Zumwalt.

Together the authors thank their families and friends who helped (or tactfully assisted) the writing of this book and the formulation of the ideas that went into it.

The authors wish, too—though not in as specific a fashion as they would prefer—to thank all the people who are working in the same field and have thereby made this book so much easier to write.

11

How This Book Will Help You

"HE IS A GOOD JUDGE OF MEN," IS ONE OF THE highest accolades we can render a man.

We can think of President Lincoln picking General Grant for the final drive of the Civil War. Or, of Sloan at General Motors, Smiddy at General Electric, and Greenewalt at DuPont surrounding themselves with the right men.

Conversely, and sadly, we remember that the reputations of President Grant and President Harding are forever shadowed because of the assistants they chose. A thousand business failures in every era testify to the mistakes that executives and managers have made in regard to whom they hired, assigned, or promoted—men who didn't "pan out."

Decisions about people are the key to decisions about sales, costs, production, finance, and whether a business progresses, stands still, or slips back. Such things don't just happen; they are caused by the actions and inactions by the people that someone—perhaps you—put in charge.

This book will help you improve or polish your natural ability to judge people; it will also sharpen your techniques and guide you into areas with which you may not be familiar. It takes the "mystique" and "amateur psychologizing" as well as the "plain fool gossip" out of making decisions, realistic decisions, about the men and women with whom you work. It does so by relating the analyses, the judgments, and decisions to the *business results* that you want to achieve.

13

It substitutes know-how and planned action for wishful thinking and vague emotionalizing.

Human relations and *scientific decision making*, until recently, have run along separate tracks. Ideas about human relations have been publicized by the sociologists, psychologists, or behavioral scientists. Theories and techniques of decision making have been promoted by the economist, statistician, and operations researcher, all of whom talk in terms of "management sciences," "alternatives," "gaming theory," and "cost effectiveness."

This book applies the techniques of decision making to human relations, but avoids the jargon, the mathematical symbols, and the formulas. It is intended for the better-than-average manager and potential executive, but is written in the language he will have to use when he deals with real people.

We recommend you read it all the way through first, because it has been constructed to form a course in the practical aspects of decision making. Having done this, you should refer more intensively to the chapters that have immediate application to your own requirements. Later, you should refer from time to time to the final chapter, to the table of contents, and to the index for quick reminders of the section of most interest to you, or which have become more important to you because of changes in your work.

If much or most of this book seems like common sense to you, good! However, the question will remain: Are you actually doing, step-by-step, the things with which you agree?

Table of Contents

15

fact analysis / Personnel facts check sheet / To sum up / A system for checking facts

chapter 11

The case of the too-high accident rate / Predictions / Actual results / Four clues to the predictions / What to do about cases of this kind / Applying the clues to other cases / What kind of clues to look for / Establish the man's modus operandi / How to understand and use motives / Affection / Submissiveness / Chart of basic motives / Dominance / Hate / Effects on others / Stan's motives: From two viewpoints / Recapitulation / Six steps to becoming a top motivator of people / Summary

chapter 12

Dealing with the under-25 group / Three checks on the young candidate / Use the credit manager's approach / Decision check list for young employees / Handling the creative employee / Creative environments may be different / Psychological profiles of cre-

man / Master and slave? / For executive attitudes / Autocratic / Bureaucratic / Technocratic / Autistic / Clues to these attitudes / Creative feedback / To understand is not to invade / Final review

improving

Your Bets on People

THIS BOOK WILL SHOW YOU HOW TO IMPROVE your "people decisions." Here's what we mean.

● When you decide on an ad campaign, you are deciding what will make *people* want your product.

● When you hire a salesman, you are deciding that he can and will get the job done.

● When you promote a man to operate a plant, you are deciding that he will produce a quality product efficiently.

These "people decisions" are so often wrong that they seem like making "bets" on what people will do. In spite of all the careful analysis, the Edsel laid an egg—the manufacturer made a wrong bet about what people wanted to drive. A costly people decision!

Advertising requires tough types of decisions. John Wanamaker said he thought half of his advertising was wasted—but he didn't know which half!

We are going to show you how you can improve your bets on people, and thereby improve all your business, because most business decisions involve people-analysis as part of the decision-making.

Why People Decisions Are So Important

If making decisions about what people will do is so much a matter of guesswork, why spend time on it?

There are four reasons why you cannot afford not to improve your bets on people:

1. The good news is that you *can* improve your ability to make people decisions—the authors have developed and proved a method for doing this!
2. You can't get away from making people decisions even if you wanted to.
3. Making people decisions is at least half the fascination of being in business.
4. Making better people decisions is the key to improving many *other* types of decisions in business.

Too many executives devote all their efforts to the *material* investments of their businesses. Yet, the *people* investments are, and always will be, the most important.

You can improve

The authors have developed a method for improving your people decisions. You will hear about it and practice it all through this book. The important thing to note here is that the method *works*.

The method, which uses a principle that engineers call "the Feedback Loop," is the simplest approach we know. You will be able to use it in this book. You will be able to apply it on the job. You will be able to use it at home, and in your social life—where there are "people decisions" to make, too.

Who has used the Feedback Method for improving people decisions? Our test groups included:

> Sales Managers
> Engineers
> Personnel Managers
> Housewives
> Ministers
> Psychologists

If they can do it, you can, too. How do we know that they were able to use the method of Feedback? Because the way the method is set up, the decision-maker automatically can learn how his decision turned out, and we can tell how often he hit the mark and how often he missed. The ratio of his hits to his misses is the decision-maker's batting average. We know that the Feedback Method did help the above groups improve their batting averages!

You can't get away from people

Executives direct managers; managers direct supervisors; and supervisors (or foremen) direct the workers or salesmen, who in turn run the machinery or handle customers. Nowhere in the organization can you find a place where you can get away from *people*.

You install a piece of equipment which will speed up production 10 per cent. Then an accident (people, again!) or a labor grievance (people!) ties it up.

The marketing department says your new product will really go. But somebody forgot to check the salesmen's attitude toward the new product. The marketing analysis was right, but the human decision was not thought through.

Most businessmen agree that *people* cause most of the headaches in business. Someone may say, "No, I think costs are the main headache." Rising costs are a headache; but it is a lack of human effort which let the costs get out of hand, and only human effort will find a way around the costs. You can't get away from people.

At least half the fascination of being in business is people. What will your competitor do if you cut the price five per cent? That's a worrisome question, and a practical one— but it is also a fascinating *people-question.*

What we are talking about in this book is the most interesting subject in the world. Even if it had nothing to do with running your business more efficiently, the subject of people would be hard to resist. Keep this in mind, because one of the cardinal rules for learning to make good bets on people is to relax and enjoy it! We will explain why that is and how you can do it—later on in this book.

People decisions are the key to other decisions

The last reason we gave for the importance of your devoting time to this book is perhaps the most vital of all: by learning to make better people decisions, you will open the door to understanding the business operation as a whole. This point is so significant that we had better explain to you exactly what we mean.

Good Decisions Are Based on Two Kinds of Analysis

Before making *any* decision in business, you make two kinds of analysis: *technical* and *personnel*. Let's think about these for a moment.

A *technical analysis* answers questions such as:

Will this new product attract new sales without cutting into our present sales volume?

Can we make money on the product if we do sell it?

Can we make the product with our present facilities?

A *personnel analysis* deals with questions such as:

Will the salesmen push the new product?

Can they learn how to handle it as fast as we are planning to get it out on the market?

Can our production department retrain its people fast enough to make this product on our schedule?

Personnel or people decisions such as these cannot be made by the personnel manager; they must be made by the line executives. Only the line executive is in a position to compare and blend the two kinds of analysis so that the personnel analysis supports the technical analysis. The proper blend produces a good business decision. Let's consider why this is so.

Your Job As a Business Forecaster

Let's consider some fundamentals. Everyone in business makes decisions. The clerk may only choose a better brand of paper clip, but that is still a decision. It is a decision which may be a poor one, just as the decision to build a new plant in South Platte County may be a poor one.

A decision is a choice among possible courses of action. A practical decision-maker chooses courses of action that actually work. He installs cooling systems that cool. He adds products to the marketing line that sell. He makes a sales presentation that persuades.

Your batting average as a decision-maker depends on how many of the courses of action you choose do actually succeed—that is, produce the *results* you wanted. The fact that you want certain results from your decisions makes you a *forecaster*, whether you like that idea or not. You are a forecaster every time you make a decision because

- The good course of action in selling is the one that gets the sales results (somebody has to make a good forecast about what will sell).
- The good course of action in negotiating is the one that obtains a favorable contract (somebody makes a good forecast about what terms to offer, and how to present them).

Most of us do not like to forecast the future. We don't want to pretend to be prophets. But life in general, particularly business life, demands success in *anticipating* what will happen. You can't cross the street without making a traffic forecast. You can't put on your clothes in the morning without making some *assumptions* about the weather. You don't make a loan before making an *estimate* of the man's ability and willingness to repay it.

Note the words used in these examples: *anticipate, forecast, assumption,* and *estimate.* The point is clear—we have to estimate the future in order to be practical.

But that's only a beginning. Success in business means the successful prediction of how other people will behave.

The Costs of People Decisions

Turnover

Suppose you make a poor prediction—select the wrong man for a job, for example. Ever figure the cost? The minimum cost of putting an unskilled man on the payroll is around $385. This figure does not include any products or machinery he may ruin or the customers he may offend before you remove him. A route salesman costs at least $1,000 to replace. An engineer costs up to $10,000 to replace. A key executive will cost more than this.

What does this mean? It means there is a definite cost figure attached to putting in a wrong man who later has to be replaced. This figure is called "turnover cost."

For example, Company X has a sales force of 1,000 men and a turnover of 10 per cent, 100 men a year. At $1,000 a man (for recruiting, formal training, on-the-job training, social security, other tax and insurance costs), the turnover cost is $100,000. If you could reduce that turnover by a slight amount—say, 10 fewer men lost a year—your direct, out-of-pocket savings would amount to $10,000.

So, pick the right men to begin with, and save a lot of money, as well as headaches.

Emotional costs

Money is not the only price we pay for making poor personnel predictions. We also pay in health: wear and tear on our nervous systems. Dr. Hans Selye, the great medical scientist, says: "Among all my autopsies (and I have performed quite a few), I have never found a man who died of old age." Dr. Selye believes that *stress* is what shortens our life spans.

How many times have you said, "If only people would do what they are supposed to do. . . ." Doesn't that statement signal exasperation and stress? It also means that your expectations—your forecasts—about the people in question were off the mark.

Improve your ability to forecast what people will do— reduce the emotional cost of doing business.

Ethical costs

Has it ever occurred to you that there is an ethical side to personnel decisions? For every headache you have because somebody did not do what you expected that he would, at least one other person also has a headache. If a man has been poorly selected for a job and does badly on it, he is not only causing you stress—think of what he is doing to himself!

Let's agree that we owe people the best decision-making of which we are capable. Honor that obligation—improve your ability to recognize other men's abilities and to contribute to their success as well as your own.

Four "Solutions" to People Failures

Someone fails to do what was expected. What to do about it? All too often, one or more of the following approaches are adopted by businessmen trying to compensate for breakdowns in human efficiency.

1. *Complaints and accusations.* The boss complains to everyone who will listen that "People just don't produce anymore." He accuses everyone but himself of being the cause of trouble. This approach stirs up more stress and spreads the infection wider and deeper into the organization.

2. *Make more rules.* The typical bureaucratic approach is to make a lot of new rules or tighten up the old ones to "ensure that the trouble never happens again." True, sometimes a revision of erroneous procedures or safety checks is required. But bureaucratic rule setting in most cases simply increases the paperwork without reaching the real sources of the trouble—the failure of the *management* to anticipate how people will perform. A business can keep adding on new rules like this for years, like a ship does barnacles, without really solving its personnel problems.

3. *Tighten the supervision.* Establishing more controls and oversupervising people is a common short-run "solution." But it means less delegation, less development for lower-ranking personnel, and more detail work for the higher echelons. It means a larger supervisory payroll, and it absorbs the time of top management so that they have no opportunity to think about business expansion and other creative subjects.

4. *Dramatic confrontation.* The boss calls in "the culprits" and "has it out with them." This practice often is the honest as well as the practical one—get the problem out in the open! But it can just as often mean that the boss is merely releasing his tensions in an emotional "blood-letting" and is failing to deal objectively with the many hidden factors behind personnel failures.

Solve the Problem by the Feedback Method

As you can surmise, we have little enthusiasm for the blind application of the approaches described above. In essence, our recommendation is:

Learn to observe other people more, and you will find yourself worrying less about yourself. Reduce the stress in your work by thinking more effectively about what others probably will do, rather than worrying about what they ought to do. As you learn to predict what others will actually do, then adapt your approach toward ensuring that what they probably will do (their probable actions) will produce the results you want.

Why do we call this the Feedback Method? Because when you actually get down to brass tacks in applying the above approach, you will find yourself checking your predictions against the facts, over and over again. Perhaps the key to the whole approach is in the very first line above: "Learn to observe other people more."

There are many reasons for observing people more. The main reason in our approach is this: The only test of your predictions is checking them against fact—actual observation of whether the approach you used does in fact obtain the results you expect.

The chapters that follow will stimulate your ability to make and test good people decisions, using the *Feedback Method,* supplemented by the method of *Forced Choices* and the method of *Personnel Gaming.* Here we will say a few words about these three methods for improving decision-making.

Feedback

Engineers use the term *feedback loop* in talking about self-correcting cycles in automation. That is, a machine checks the quality of its own output and then adjusts its settings as necessary.

In dealing with human beings, it is difficult to get the information which would provide us feedback in the right form and at the right time. This means that if we are wrong in our expectations or judgment of a person, we often do not know it. We therefore cannot correct our own impressions.

This is why so few of us improve in the handling of people over a period of years. Feedback is the vital factor in learning from experience. Can a deaf man learn to play the piano? No, because he has to hear how the notes sound. Could you become an expert marksman if you could not check the target to see where your shots were hitting? Obviously, no.

Yet thousands of executives, managers, and supervisors make decisions about people with no follow-up, no feedback. Sometimes they are just too lazy or dense to use the feedback that is available. But in most instances, their organizations do not provide the feedback data in proper form, or not soon enough.

Our approach is to provide you plenty of prompt feedback in a form designed for your immediate use. Then we will show you how you can build this method into the way your own job is organized and how you can apply it to your social and family life.

Forced choices

What we call "forced choices" here is often termed *business gaming*. That is, you learn by doing—by being required to make a decision and then seeing what happens.

If a businessman actually used some experimental new approaches in his organization, the place would fall apart! So he tries "gaming" the various approaches. Using computers and expert guidance, a group of executives can "play the game," making decisions about how to apply business resources to exploit specific opportunities, operating under particular limitations. Then the machines quickly spew back the figures showing how their decisions "maximized" the profits or "minimized" the costs.

In short, the executives learn from the business game just as generals learn from the war game; they go through all the maneuvers to see what result they would have, but the ammunition is not live.

Personnel gaming

In the management training program known as business gaming, you make decisions and find out quickly what happens. But you do this without the risk of making the decision in real life.

Why not apply the same approach to problems about people? The "personnel decision-making game" is based on years of testing—testing of the principles, techniques, and results of the approach. Learn to make the decisions called for in this book, and you will find yourself increasingly able to handle the people problems you will find in real life.

To Sum Up

All business decisions ultimately involve people decisions. The technical analyses and technical planning are basic, of course; but whatever the technical decision is, it must be carried out by people.

Unfortunately, it is difficult, and sometimes impossible, to disentangle the human elements from all the other elements of a situation. Instead of making a forecast of how the people will probably react to or carry out the chosen course of action, the manager all too often forecasts what he thinks the people *ought* to do or what he *wants* them to do.

This book teaches you to improve your forecasting of what people will do. Since that will improve the human aspect of your decision-making, your decision-making "batting average" should improve and the emotional cost you pay for doing business should be reduced. That is, stress (emotional strain) is produced when people do not do what you expect them to do.

The learning process teaches you to analyze people and predict what they will do. You will go through a carefully designed series of "people decisions." As you make those decisions, you will be completing a course in "personnel gaming."

The decisions will be yours. But we will provide you with the "feedback" which indicates whether the decision has the effect you expected.

Can you raise your batting average? We are sure that you can. Let's get started!

how to

Make Hiring Decisions

WE SAW A COMPANY GAIN A PROFIT INCREASE OF $1,000,000 in *one plant in one year* by selecting the right plant manager. We've also seen many, many run-of-the-mill situations where men and women were happy or unhappy, effective or ineffective, simply because of the persons they selected to work for them.

You can earn next year, let's say, an additional $100,000 in sales by putting the right salesman in the territory.

You may want to know if Bob Fenster is the "right man" for a particular job, but your sales manager is "too busy" to spend more than 30 minutes interviewing him. Is thirty minutes all he can spare for a hundred thousand dollar decision?

Obviously, we need some yardsticks for deciding how much time one *must* afford to spend in such matters. This chapter will explain five fundamental principles on which to base hiring decisions.

The first principle is:

> *I. It's easier and cheaper to pick the right man for a job than to train the wrong man to do the job!*

37

The second principle is:

II. Recognize the dollar value of successful hiring and devote time in proportion to the job's importance.

Mr. Al Hansen, the personnel manager in a Chicago factory, boasted to us that he had picked his new production foreman "in only 20 minutes!" We asked him, "How much did you *risk* in this decision?"

He didn't know what we were talking about. We went on to express concern that he had not spent at least two hours—at a minimum—in talking with the new man and checking into his past performances.

Mr. Hansen said, "Well, I don't have two hours for that! I hire—and fire—quickly."

That's part of the trouble with the word *hiring*. It conjures up images of the old-fashioned bull-of-the-woods foreman who hires men from a labor shape-up. He would look at the men and snarl: "I'll take *You* and *You* and *You*. The rest go on home and come back tomorrow."

Professional decisions about people take thought—and are worth it. Think of the expert doctor pondering a diagnosis or a highly paid attorney working up a legal brief. These reflect the image of professional decision-making we have in mind for all executives, managers, and foremen.

Three ways to calculate the value of hiring

Suppose a foreman will be paid $10,000 a year. In the industry in question the average foreman stays on the job for 20 years. You may, therefore, invest $200,000 when you hire him. That is one way to figure the value of the hiring.

A second way already mentioned is to estimate the additional sales or production expected. The dollar value of hiring a salesman who will bring an additional $100,000 is obviously 100,000 times the years projected ahead.

A third way is to divide the company profits by the number of employees. For example, a company employs 5,000 men and earns $20,000,000 in profits. Each man represents a potential annual $4,000 profit package to you!

These are obviously not financial yardsticks, nor can we compare our "$200,000 foreman" with the "$100,000 salesman." But these yardsticks do express hiring as a business function that will repay time and effort.

Compare your present hiring practices with these yardsticks. Are you satisfied?

Yardsticks for Interview Time

Relatively brief consideration can be given to the "also-rans"—the large number of persons who want a job but do not reach the "finals." The finalists, and especially the last one of all, are the ones we are talking about.

There are two key factors: (1) the value or risk of the position to be filled, and (2) the improvement in the decision-making which you can gain by devoting more time. The law of diminishing returns applies: after a certain number of interview hours, additional hours provide nothing new.

The rule we have found most useful is: *provide an hour's appraisal time for every $2,000 in salary the job pays, up to the first $20,000 a year. For the next $20,000 add an hour's*

*appraisal for every $1,000 in salary. Beyond $40,000, add an
hour's appraisal for each $500 in salary.* For example:

POSITION	ANNUAL SALARY	MINIMUM INTERVIEW TIME
Salesman	$ 8,000	4 hours
Engineer	12,000	6 hours
Sales Manager	16,000	8 hours
Comptroller	30,000	20 hours
President	50,000	50 hours

III. *Check the results of past hiring practices.*

How do you check results in hiring? One company president, Mr. David L. MacKinnon, followed the practice of
approving all executive staff additions from outside the company. He finally accepted our recommendation to check
the results of his decisions on the 27 such key men he had
approved during the past five years.

Mr. MacKinnon studied their performance records for
the five-year period. He had his secretary make the following
tabulations:

1. How many of the men were still with the company?
2. How many of those who had left had done so because
    they had failed?
3. How many of those still with the company were doing
    outstanding work?

He found that 20 of the men were still with the company; 7 had left under fire; none had left because of better
job offers.

Mr. MacKinnon began asking some searching questions: What had been overlooked during the hiring procedures? In which instances had a careless decision been made? Could the errors be avoided in the future?

He asked questions, too, about the 20 still with the company. How many of them were really productive? How many were coasting? How many remained as awkward monuments to executive pride that would not admit an error in selecting?

Analyzing the Results

Mr. MacKinnon found that 6 of the 20 still with the company had in some way proved disappointing. Only 14 of the original 27 were really doing the jobs for which they had been selected. In other words, his hiring methods were about 50 per cent effective! In baseball, a .500 batting average is fantastically good; but in business, is it good enough? These were questions Mr. MacKinnon raised.

Mr. MacKinnon reviewed some notes he had jotted down at the various hirings. For example, his notes on Bill Nabor included the following:

> Nabor should make us a good manufacturing engineer. He has had experience heading a company—the Blackman Company in Detroit—which went bankrupt last year because of competitive conditions in his market over which he had no control. One of the letters of reference says, "Nabor is a good engineer and manager, though we have heard he hits the bottle now and then."

"Hits the bottle!" Mr. MacKinnon exploded: "Why didn't we follow that up?" Mr. MacKinnon had known plenty of men who had been on the bottle during some part of their lives, but had recovered to do good work. However, he had failed to make sure Nabor could control any drinking. What had happened?

Nabor hadn't been on the job in MacKinnon's company a month before someone remarked that Bill smelled of alcohol even before lunch.

Nabor had not admitted a drinking problem and had not sought or accepted help. He had not lasted a year.

Then there was Tom Wilson, an attorney, who had lasted only four months. Mr. MacKinnon's notes written at the time he had hired Wilson were:

> Wilson does not appear to have a strong personality but is qualified in tax work and has the technical knowledge we want. The Accounting Manager thinks he can do the job. Wilson will accept the lower pay limit, and I like the idea of holding the payrolls low at this time.

"Can do the job"—just barely, it turned out! Wilson turned out to be a listless quitter, browbeaten by job failures.

Poor Wilson! But why had he been hired? Apparently the phrase used—"can do the job"—meant that the company had set out to obtain a mediocrity and had obtained one. Then they found they needed more than minimum qualifications and they had let Wilson go in less than 10 months.

Mr. MacKinnon realized he was learning some important things about his organization by making his *results-survey*. In particular, he saw the significance of our fourth principle:

IV. An organization reveals the value it places on people by the thoroughness with which it hires them.

After going through the other cases, Mr. MacKinnon found not only more instances of lax decision-making, but also a lot of good thinking and good decisions. He drew up a "profit and loss" sheet for the past hiring decisions:

On the profit side he wrote:

1. We did well in selecting when we had agreed on the need for a high type of man.
2. We did well in selecting when we checked thoroughly into the man's history, education, efforts to improve himself, and his personality.
3. The men we selected who later turned out well were usually men who left a very favorable impression in three of these four areas. Our very top three men had favorable indications in all four of these areas of appraisal.

On the loss side he wrote:

1. Our major errors occurred because we did not insist on following up any misgivings. Had we done so we might have averted 8 of the 13 bad decisions.
2. In five instances, the man might have made the grade had we handled him and our office politics better.
3. In four cases we did not estimate correctly the work the new executive should do.

What Not to Do

What should a man in Mr. MacKinnon's position do after such a post-mortem? Here are four paths he ought NOT to take:

1. Write a memorandum scolding all department heads for their past selections and point out that costs of hiring and firing seven of the men had amounted to over $70,000. Then write another blast against the departments that had the six men on the payroll who were not fully producing.

2. Call in the Personnel Department and demand that they tighten up or install all sorts of hiring rules to prevent future errors, such as failing to check references doubly or even triply.

3. Require all his top men to involve themselves in all the hiring steps.

4. Reprimand and harass individuals most responsible for the wrong hiring decisions; i.e., really bear down on whoever was at fault.

These four approaches, of course, represent the all-too-common reactions to poor decisions about people which we described in the previous chapter. They are

1. Complaints and accusations
2. Bureaucratic rule-making
3. Confronting the culprits
4. Tightening up supervision (oversupervision)

A Total Approach That Worked

Mr. MacKinnon did something else, and that "something else" is what this book is about. He did call in his personnel manager and his department heads, and he did give them firm guidance. In substance, it was this:

> This company was built on results—and it's the way we must follow to stay in business. I have checked some of the results of 27 personnel decisions which I have made during the past few years and found that my success average was only 50 per cent. I want you to study your own decisions about people for a similar period. If you did better than I, congratulations! If not, you had better join me in seeing where we are going wrong and what we can do to ensure better "people results." I intend to improve my average. I want you to do the same.

This example leads us to our fifth principle:

> V. *Every executive and manager should*
> *regularly review his hiring results.*

Selection Results Feedback

Mr. MacKinnon, in effect, established a *feedback* system such as we described in Chapter 1. In engineering we say that a machine which checks the quality of its own output and adjusts its settings as required employs a "feedback loop."

Let's consider the *feedback system* that Mr. MacKinnon planned to introduce into his company. He did the following:

1. He used what doctors call "consecutive records." That is, he took *all* the cases in a particular period, and did not leave out the ones he would rather forget!

2. He took an honest, hard look at the present status of each man, and classified him as: (a) still with the company but not doing an outstanding job; (b) still with the company and highly productive; (c) not with the company because of his own choice; or (d) not with the company at the company's choice.

3. He summarized his total success—or batting average— for all 27 cases.

4. He accepted his share of responsibility for the decisions he had approved.

5. He analyzed the causes for the effective and ineffective decisions, and drew up a profit and loss sheet to dramatize his findings.

Page 47 illustrates a Hiring Results Summary Check List which can help you review your past record as a personnel selection decision-maker. But the review of the past is only the starting point for analyzing the factors that underlie successful decisions about people in modern business. The important parts of a true feedback system are the steps that correct the "settings" in the feedback loop. Let's begin by appraising Mr. MacKinnon's approach, then consider some of the things all executives ought to know or do.

Hiring Results Summary and Check List

NAME	POSITION AND DEPARTMENT	DATE OF HIRE	STILL WITH COMPANY	YEARS ON JOB	HOW PRODUCTIVE	REASON HE LEFT	HIRING ERRORS
Bill Nabor	Engineering Supervisor	1959	No	½	Poor	Discharged for drinking	Failed to check reference to drink
Tom Wilson	Tax Attorney	1960	No	¾	Mediocre	Encouraged to resign	Tried to save money by hiring below true needs
Dave Scott	Product Manager	1960	Yes	—	Excellent	—	—
L. Atkinson	Engineering Design Manager	1961	No	2	Only fair	Encouraged to resign	Overlooked his difficulties in supervising others
Jerry Wright	Eastern Division Production Manager	1962	Yes	—	Mediocre	—	Did not get clear definition of job before we hired him
Robert Dix	Patent Attorney	1963	Yes	—	Good	—	Should have insisted on more experience
J. M. Walmsley	North Central Sales Manager	1963	No	1	Only fair	Discharged for inability to follow policies	Should have checked his job-hopping pattern
Etc.	Etc.	Etc.	Etc.	Etc.	Etc.	Etc.	Etc.
TOTALS			20 (Yes) 7 (No)		14 (productive) 6 (not productive)	0 (left voluntarily) 7 (left involuntarily)	

Critique of MacKinnon's Approach

We like Mr. MacKinnon's honesty, his appreciation of the importance of good hiring, and his effort to involve his department heads. However, he did not go far enough into the problem in four key respects:

1. *Motivation*: More shake-up of the managers' attitudes toward hiring would be necessary. One memo would not be enough to instill a results-centered attitude toward hiring. A prolonged effort will be needed.

2. *Specific feedback*: Much more needs to be known in regard to the successes and failures of the men. We need to know how each man performed in relation to the predictions made about him at the time he was hired. Perhaps the man's success was accidental and did not reflect good hiring judgment. Perhaps failure was due to factors other than poor performance.

3. *Simulation*: Analysis of past decisions is important, but we can't change the past. Our task is to improve the future. The ground for this can be laid by training and particularly by simulation methods. (More about these later.)

4. *Interpersonal relations*: Truly useful feedback studies help one learn the interpersonal factors that lead to success or failure. Such studies also often reveal that improved interpersonal relationships between the man hired and his boss can prevent the failures, thus raising the hiring "batting average." Conversely, poor human relations lower the batting average.

Management Training in Hiring

You might say, "Our personnel department does all the hiring, so what's all this to me?" Well, few, if any, personnel departments do all the hiring. Even when they play the major part, others are involved in the decisions to hire, to promote, and to transfer personnel. Finally, many decisions that you *do* make about people will benefit from your knowledge of the basic principles of sound hiring.

You should, therefore, start out by repeating President MacKinnon's method—at your own desk—if at all possible. Find out what your batting average has been.

Then, use the cases that follow to test and develop your skill in analyzing and deciding whom to hire. As you analyze your batting average keep the five principles in mind:

I. It's easier and cheaper to pick the right man for a job than to train the wrong man to do the job!

II. Recognize the dollar value of successful hiring and devote time in proportion to the job's importance.

III. Check the results of past hiring practices.

IV. An organization reveals the value it places on people by the thoroughness with which it hires them.

V. Every executive and manager should regularly review his hiring results.

how to

Analyze Promotion Potential

MANAGING A BUSINESS DEMANDS A VIGOROUS BUT balanced approach that puts the right man in the right job. A business executive, like a general, has to control the deployment of his men. An ancient military principle states that the side with the best reserve troops will prevail. In business, a similar principle applies: each new generation or "platoon" of managers must be kept moving forward—but not too close on the heels of those ahead of them!

The Three Types of Analysis
Required

You should make three types of analysis before you assign, re-assign, or promote a man. These are: (1) technical business analysis, (2) organization analysis, and (3) personnel analysis.

The technical analysis answers the question, Does the job itself need to be done?

The organization analysis answers the question, Where and by whom should the work be done?

51

The personnel analysis answers the question about the man, "Can Jones do the job?"

Technical Analysis

The board of directors of a corporation manufacturing consumer goods (sales volume $80 million a year, mainly in the eastern half of the United States) realized that its competitors had surpassed it in new product development. The board pressed for product research, and the president responded by establishing a product research department.

However, each corporate officer had a different idea of what the product research department should do. The manufacturing vice-president wanted new products tested for costs on the production line. The marketing manager wanted packages tested. The advertising manager wanted the new department to poll consumers, and so on.

The company executives had never before spent money on product research. The new budget ($150,000, the first year) looked like a lot of money to them, and they reasoned that they'd get a lot for it. "After all," as the advertising manager said, "that hundred and fifty thousand comes out of all our budgets—especially mine—and we ought to have something to show for it."

The president picked Everett Fox to be head of the new product research department. Though only 43, Everett had had production-line experience and knew manufacturing inside and out. He was intelligent, expressed himself clearly and vigorously, and radiated enthusiasm.

But before the end of the year, he had drawn the fire of the other department heads. "He is not producing," they said. The president was ill at that time and not in touch with the situation. Therefore, when all of his top executives advised, "Get rid of Everett," the President felt he had to take action.

What Went Wrong?

It is easy to see that the trouble started when the company failed to decide what was most wanted from the product research department. Top management violated the basic business principle—*Be clear about your objectives.*

Perhaps the conflicting demands placed on Everett Fox could have been met had he been provided with adequate resources—men, materials, money, and time. Compare his budget to the average research and development expenditure in the United States that amounts to 3, 5, or even 10 per cent of gross sales (depending on the industry). Fox's budget was $150,000—or about two-tenths of one per cent of gross sales—and it should have been at least a million dollars, especially for a company starting so late in research and development.

The moral of this story is that technical business analysis ought to be done properly before one starts to analyze Everett Fox; first, as a potential department head; and second, as a success or failure in his year on the job. Here's the principle:

*I. Before delegating work, decide (a)
how much it is actually needed, and then
decide (b) how much to invest in getting*

it done (be sure it is enough), based on what you want from it. These are technical business questions.

Organizational Analysis

Let's look at the errors inherent in the way authority and responsibility were delegated to Everett Fox. Storm warnings showed in the attitudes of the department heads and the storm broke over Fox when his "patron," the president, became ill.

It was obvious that:

• Fox had been directed to report to the president in order to have adequate authority. But this was wrongly interpreted to mean to report *only* to the president. Fox did not report frequently enough to convey and resolve his real problems; then later, he could not because the president was sick.

• Fox should have had monthly conferences with the other department heads to review the plans and progress of product research. This would have provided an outlet for the criticisms and provided opportunities for rescheduling or at least explaining the projects and priorities.

Here is our second principle:

II. An organization analysis should be made to establish where a job belongs in a company's structure, with whom it

must be coordinated, and what commu-
nications must be maintained.

Personnel Analysis

The President of the company realized that more than
Everett's performance was at fault. As a temporary measure,
he appointed Mr. Larsen, Vice President for International
Marketing, to head a research coordinating committee. The
committee's first task was to review the progress of the product research department and *to approve all requests made
to it.*

But Mr. Larsen found the job of mediating the demands
of the different departments an unpleasant one; he believed
that other company matters were more urgent. So, he held
only one meeting of the committee and thereafter was "too
busy." Why? Because Mr. Larsen, having built his position
through some astute international trading transactions, pre-
ferred to spend his time outside the corporate offices dealing
with international traders in dignified negotiations (which
did contribute to the success of the company as well as to
his own reputation). In short, he remained a full-time marketing executive and did not become a research coordinating
executive. Mr. Larsen had the ability to do the job, but not
the motivation to do it.

Now, we are ready for the third principle of personnel
analysis:

> *III. After you have established by tech-*
> *nical and organizational analyses what*
> *work ought to be done and how it should*

be done, then you decide who can *and*
will *do it.*

Price Out the Qualities You Want

The vaguer and more intangible the personnel values
of qualities that you desire, the more objective and calculat-
ing you should be in your approach to measuring them. Of
course, you don't measure "leadership," "enthusiasm," "motivational power," "creativity," in the same way you can
measure a man's output of widgets on a milling machine or
a salesman's ability to write up sales orders. But that simply
means you must try all the harder.

One good method, recommended by Joseph G. Mason*,
is to put a price tag on the qualities you are seeking. Here's
how Mr. Mason explains his method:

> . . . assume that these characteristics can be purchased
> in any quantities for 10 cents each. You have $10 to
> spend. How would you shop for them—how much would
> you spend on each of the characteristics you think are
> important?

> When you have done this, look over your list. If you
> decide to spend $2.50 on "Technical Knowledge" and
> $1.25 on "Administrative Ability," think this through.
> What you are saying is that you consider technical
> knowledge to be twice as important as administrative
> ability. Do you really mean that? Possibly you do, but
> one of the prime advantages of putting values on your

---

* Joseph G. Mason, "New Way to Improve Your Decisions," *Nation's
Business*, June 1964.

thoughts is that you have the opportunity of studying unrelated factors on a common basis. This may lead to better decision-making.

This pricing-out method is particularly useful when you are dealing with a group that has to pass on the selection. Each member of the group will see the man's qualifications in a different way. But when you get each one to put a price tag on the qualifications, you will find that you can quickly bring them into agreement on the "value" of the characteristics they are looking for.

For the purposes of our discussion in this chapter and the succeeding chapters, we will use the rating scale—simple? yes; tried-and-true? yes; and for those reasons, safely employable here.

The Four Basic Factors to Be Sure to Rate

The four factors listed below are so obviously the basic ones that no further explanation for them need be given— particularly to the type of reader who will be using this book. They are:

	Scale to Be Used					
	Highest	*High*	*Av.*	*Below Av.*	*Too Low*	
INTELLIGENCE	6	5	4	3	2	1
DRIVE, PERSISTENCE	6	5	4	3	2	1
HUMAN RELATIONS, PERSUASIVENESS	6	5	4	3	2	1
MATURITY, PERSONALITY	6	5	4	3	2	1

Let's apply them in some real-life cases.

The Ken Harold Problem

Ken Harold, 42, has had a great deal of experience in a large firm that manufactures hard goods. He moved from one department to another, doing a good job in each and gaining well-rounded experience. He finished near the top in a company-sponsored executive training program. Yet, the company is reluctant to make him the manager of one of its plants.

We examined his case and found the main complaint about him to be: "He doesn't look or sound like a manager. He's too fat, and he dresses badly." Apparently the company wants a man who looks like a man of distinction and who can at the same time maintain the respect of the hard-nosed producers in the factory. It also wants a man who can sell in the front offices of major customers and convince them of his plant's ability to render good service on a schedule. However, several people believe that Ken probably could not supervise people or sell himself to customers. Ken appears to have the following qualities:

Ken Harold

	Scale Rating
	High Low
INTELLIGENCE: He has a well-rounded knowledge of plant operations; he learns quickly and certainly can pick up quickly what he needs to know about customers.	6 (5) 4 3 2 1
DRIVE, AGGRESSIVENESS, and PERSISTENCE: He gets things done. Extremely ambitious; will probably leave the company if not given a better assignment.	(6) 5 4 3 2 1

INTERPERSONAL ABILITY: He is quiet,   6 5 4 (3) 2 1
stands well in the eyes of company executives, but lacks record of personal
salesmanship successes.

EMOTIONAL MATURITY: Stolid and confi-   6 (5) 4 3 2 1
dent; good family life; does not upset
under pressure.

The job of plant manager for which Ken is being considered demands high aggressiveness, average business intelligence, at least average emotional stability, and considerable persuasiveness and salesmanship. Of course, there can
be trade-offs. High strength in one area can offset weaknesses
in other areas—so long as there is a plan to bolster the weaknesses.

The Recommendation? Ken can handle the job, and in
the absence of a better candidate, he should be given the
opportunity. However, he should be helped to learn to sell
and he should have a strong sales manager to assist him.

The Results? From the outset, Ken did well in the area
of cost reduction and in improving production and administration. Improvements in sales, as was to be expected, were
slow; but his internal economies caused profits to rise stead-
ily, and the helps given him to build a new sales force prom-
ised to pay off in the future.

Which to Promote: Woodson
or Studebaker?

Keith Woodson and Bill Studebaker were two top manufacturing engineers, either of whom logically could step up

to take the place of Chief Manufacturing Engineer Nick Davis, who because of ill health was retiring at 59, three years ahead of the usual retirement date.

Bill Studebaker, 44, had been the second man in the department and had worked for Davis for 12 years. It was generally assumed he would replace Davis.

Keith Woodson, 34, had been employed by the company for five years and had been in a different plant location most of the time. It was difficult to compare the performance of the two men, not only because of the physical distance, but also because in the area where Keith was stationed the plants were clustered so Keith could give prompt and direct attention to manufacturing problems—something Bill's situation had made it difficult for him to do. Otherwise, it appeared their performance was comparable in terms of actual results.

Nick Davis decided to choose his successor on the basis of each man's potential for higher responsibilities. Keith, the younger man, had his strong suit in overall aggressiveness and persistence in getting the job done. At the same time, he seemed to be extremely well-liked; his people followed him without question.

Keith Woodson

	Scale Rating
	High Low
INTELLIGENCE: Sound but not brilliant	6 5 (4) 3 2 1
DRIVE: Gets the job done!	6 (5) 4 3 2 1
HUMAN RELATIONS: Well-liked	6 (5) 4 3 2 1
PERSONALITY: Emotionally stable	6 (5) 4 3 2 1

Bill Studebaker

	Scale Rating
	High Low
INTELLIGENCE: Knows the business: what he has learned, but learns new things slowly.	6 5 4 (3) 2 1
DRIVE: Gets the job done, though does not put the drive into it that Keith does.	6 5 (4) 3 2 1
HUMAN RELATIONS: Quiet, "neutral" personality; strikes everyone as highly reliable.	6 (5) 4 3 2 1
PERSONALITY: Able to sell what he is really familiar with.	6 5 4 (3) 2 1

Nick Davis decided that Keith had more potential to adapt and to lead in the future; whereas, to choose Bill would be simply rewarding past loyalty. So, Nick passed over his old friend Bill and selected Keith as his successor. Eventually, even Bill came to recognize (if not enjoy) the rightness of the decision.

(Note that Nick Davis did not let his choice be affected by two circumstances which all too often are given too much weight: (1) "Good old Bill Studebaker" was well-known because he worked in the same area, but Keith Woodson worked at a distance; (2) "It would be expensive in travel expenses and related costs to move Keith for the promotion, while there would be no such expense in promoting Bill." All too often, people do the apparently easy thing and promote the man already at hand. However, breaking up the qualifications and rating them one by one, as Nick Davis did here, you identify the important ones and you avoid the effects of bias.

Let's apply this principle in a problem taken from real life.

The Bailey Retirement Problem

Mr. Bailey, 63, had been one of the founding fathers of a large dry goods retail chain. In particular, he set up its internal organization and for 25 years has been Financial Vice-President. Five years ago, his hope of becoming the next company president was thwarted, and he settled into a rut. His critics claim he has done nothing to improve his department in recent years. However, they can't point to any problems in the department—at least, not any operating problems. The reports are on time; the budget forecasts are on the target; and Mr. Bailey's business advice is uniformly good, if conservative.

Mr. Bailey has done little to develop a successor. He has shown some preference toward Tom Monahan, 32, giving him the special projects. However, Mr. Bailey has not given Tom any supervisory experience, and the other executives know little about Tom and naturally question his ability to succeed Bailey.

The morale in Mr. Bailey's department is only fair. Some of the employees grumble that they can't see a future in the company. He does not encourage his subordinates to obtain further education, because he is opposed to company help for anyone's advancement efforts. Our problem is: What should be done about Mr. Bailey?

Our analysis of Mr. Bailey's strengths and weaknesses is based on what the other executives tell us and on our own interviews with Mr. Bailey. We make the following ratings:

Comment and Supporting Evidence: Mr. Bailey

	Scale Rating
	High *Low*
INTELLIGENCE: Intelligent and knowledgeable but only in his specialty.	6 (5) 4 3 2 1
DRIVE: Has had the capacity for aggressiveness but has settled into a rut.	6 5 4 (3) 2 1
HUMAN RELATIONS: Is unwilling to negotiate differences with certain department heads and has built up dislikes with some; with others he remains friendly, going with them on frequent fishing trips.	6 5 4 3 (2) 1
PERSONALITY: Can sell others when he wants but rarely makes the effort.	6 5 4 3 (2) 1

Mr. Bailey's colleagues respect his intellectual ability in the area of financial management. His weakness in the other areas explains why he was not advanced to the presidency. Probably, at one time, he was stronger in drive but succumbed to the disappointments of his career. (Remember, he is being rated in terms of a vice-president's qualifications; his scores would be much higher if he were a branch or section head.)

What would you recommend be done with Mr. Bailey?

[   ] Give him early retirement?

[   ] Demote him?

[   ] Arrange for the President to work more
closely with him, as a
morale boost; see how
he reacts?

[   ] Retire him but keep
as consultant?

[   ] Arrange for expand-
ed responsibilities?

[   ] Leave him alone—
he is doing his job?

In real life, the company tried to "retread" him by putting him on a company committee whose members were all
much younger. The President thought that this would enable
Mr. Bailey to make wider contributions to policy-making
outside his specialty and at the same time the contact with
younger minds would stimulate him.

Mr. Bailey's first contributions to the committee were
excellent, thus making the President feel he had done a wise
thing in expanding Mr. Bailey's responsibilities. However,
Mr. Bailey suddenly felt he had "lost face" because he was
assigned to a "junior committee." He quit attending the
meetings.

The President gave him the option of resigning and con-
tinuing to serve as a consultant, or taking immediate retirement. He chose the latter, bitterly refusing to admit that he
in any way merited the treatment.

However, in the few weeks before he left, and to everyone's surprise but the President's, Mr. Bailey worked hard
to prepare the way for his successor, probably Tom Mona-

han, and his department was in excellent shape at the time of his departure.

Look again at Mr. Bailey's record and at his personnel analysis. He had been one of the "early giants of the company," and he had above average intelligence and drive—not enough to have made him president, but so much so that he turned sour and cynical when thwarted. But the challenge to his pride to "build a monument before he left" had motivated him to do his best to leave his department in the "best damn condition possible." This, of course, included plans for employee development, overhaul of systems, analysis of methods and policies, and so on—all the things Mr. Bailey had allowed to go by the board during his years of disappointment. However, the President also realized that Bailey's new burst of energy would be limited, being directly related to his termination date and to his pride in immediate results. To have kept him with the company longer—note Bailey's low marks in Human Relations and Personality—would have simply meant re-establishing the slump he and his department had been in before.

To Sum Up

Before you decide to promote or select a man (including yourself!), you should make three separate analyses, trying not to let the one blur your vision of the other. These are:

1. A *technical* analysis of the nature of the job and of its requirements.
2. An *organizational* analysis to establish agreement in regard to where the job belongs. In which de-

partment? Reporting to whom? In close coordination with whom?

3. A *personnel* analysis, which should come *after* the other analyses, and which should analyze the candidates in terms of their demonstrated patterns of intelligence and knowledge, drive and aggressiveness, human relations and inter-personal abilities, and their persuasiveness or salesmanship.

Oddly enough, the really difficult part about making accurate, valid analyses—ones that come true in real life—is your decision to do so. Once you decide to try, and after you make the effort to establish the three analysis areas (technical, organizational, personnel), you will find the evidence begins to sort itself out and to make sense. Moreover, you will find that your batting average will be better than you expected; and that as time goes by, you will find the great majority of your personnel decisions will prove them accurate beyond even your own hopes. This is true because, (1) Human beings follow patterns—they repeat themselves; (2) Men are pretty good judges of each other's potential—particularly when they follow the practices described in this chapter that cause them to systematize, to collect, to arrange, and to display the data in ways that facilitate decision making.

how to

Forecast What
People Will Do

Why Forecasting Is Necessary

You can learn to forecast what people will do—and that's not just a promise to teach you magic! You have to predict how a customer will respond to a new product or how your seniors will react to a proposed change. You make forecasts and predictions every day of your life, and make them successfully. When you cross the street at a traffic light, you rely on the law-abiding qualities of car drivers; you predict that they will stop.

When you bring flowers home on your wedding anniversary you are predicting they will please your wife. When you say, "Henry Jones will make a first-rate candidate for governor," you are predicting his political performance. When a hot-rodder passes you doing 85 on a 40-mile-an-hour highway, you expect him to run into trouble of some kind. A few miles further you see him showing his license to a state patrolman: forecast confirmed.

No action in business is taken without an expectation of results. No action affecting *people* should be taken without a positive expectation of results—forecasting and predicting what the people will do and how they will behave. Let's boil the difficulties of people-predicting into five basic rules or steps and build our discussion around them.

The Five Basic Steps to Personnel Forecasts

1. Make up *your* own mind that the forecasts are necessary, possible, and that you can and will make them.

2. Decide what or which *results* you must or want to predict.

3. Decide on and describe the job specifications for the *type* of man who is needed to obtain the results.

4. Match the *qualifications* of the available men against the specifications of the job.

5. If a perfect match or fit cannot be obtained, work out a back-up plan to *bolster* the man's weak points.

The importance of making up your mind

Making up your mind in regard to forecasting what other people will do means that you energize yourself to make the effort and to clarify just what you are going to forecast.

It is human to fear to stick one's neck out. While all business decisions predict the future, people usually prefer not to mention, much less emphasize this point, lest they be held up for scorn. However, the sooner you admit that you are always betting on people—not on money, or raw materials, or machinery, or real estate, or interest rates, but on the people who use the things—the sooner you admit it to yourself, the sooner you can clarify your thinking and your deciding.

First off, you distinguish between the things you can control and those that will control you; between the things the man or men you are deciding about can control and those that will control them. Too many people confuse these; they waste energy trying to shape events beyond their power, or they fail to control where they can affect events but do not know they can, or do not try to do so. For example, one might accurately forecast the growth of air freight throughout the world, even though he cannot affect the tremendous trend himself. However, one can predict that certain areas of the world will need more airport facilities within 10 years, and he can be ready to get 30 per cent of the contracts. Or, one predicts that an air-freight legal expert will be needed, and he encourages young Mike Corrigan to study transportation law.

In short, when you face a personnel decision, you must realize that it involves predicting the controllable future; i.e., what the future environment will be outside your sphere and outside your control, and also what will be the consequences of the various decisions available to you. Facing the future element, the forecast element, of any decision is the key step, yet most of us find many ways of avoiding even admitting it exists!

Decide the results
you must predict

When you start to hire or assign a man, ask yourself: "What results do I expect him to obtain?" Note that this is more pointed than just asking: "Is he the right man? Or, "What will he do?" He can be and do a lot of things, ranging from hard-nosed actions to mollycoddling ones, from playing the busy-body to do-nothing. But what results do you expect to obtain?

Moreover, you should put the results into quantitative terms to the greatest extent possible. You are selecting a man who will, for example:

> • Raise sales an average of 7 per cent a year, and achieve within five years a total increase of about 40 per cent, which will be by that time a 16 per cent share of the market in his area.

> • Cut costs absolutely by $50,000 within the next 3 years and ensure that the cost ratios of his department compare closely with industry-wide averages.

> • Hire six strong new men over the next four years and permit or facilitate the retirement of two who are reaching the company's prescribed retirement age, and two more whose production has slid off.

> • Increase office production by 5 per cent while reducing clerical turnover from 30 per cent to 20 per cent and cutting absenteeism by 25 per cent.

Note how operating forecasts like the foregoing require you and the other executives involved to decide what sort of personnel forecasts they are going to make. You can't hire a man on the basis that he's going to double sales when the total market would permit even Superman to increase sales only 5 per cent. Nor can you expect a new production assistant to cut costs by $100,000 when the materials involved cost 90 per cent of that amount, and their price is established by an international cartel.

But you can, and should, force yourself to be result-conscious. Establish the results that are feasible, then think about the type of man, or men, who can best obtain them for you.

Establish the job specs

After you have agreed on the results you want, your next step is to establish the job specifications.

Warning. Don't write these like the Civil Service or corporation "Position Descriptions" and "Job Descriptions" that are filled with vague generalities like:

> The incumbent shall display significant measures of high-level judgment in his liaison with important personnel. He shall maintain a satisfactory rate of technological advancement and shall regularly review the literature for pertinent facilities, equipment or methodology. By means of appropriate psychological and other incentives, he will incentivate his subordinates . . . and so forth.

The job specifications are the qualities and abilities that the man will have to have in order to achieve the results you want. As long as you keep the "specs" tied to the "results," you will avoid the "incumbent" phraseology—and plain nonsense—shown in the example above. Try to keep your approach along the following lines:

A. EXAMPLE OF A PRODUCTION JOB

Results Desired	Job Specs
a. Reduce materials handling costs to meet competition; i.e., by 11.5 per cent.	a. Knowledge of conveyor belts, job simplification, gravity drops, fork lifts, linear programing.
b. Speed up production by 13 per cent on standard items and reduce delays on special orders.	b. Ability to sell cost consciousness, set example, maintain quality in a department of 250 workers, 35 per cent of whom are skilled women assemblers.
c. Replace equipment in accordance with 5-year master depreciation and obsolescence plan.	c. Willingness (and family conditions) to stay at least 6 years to repay cost of training and on-the-job preparation.
And so on . . .	And so on . . .

B. EXAMPLE OF A SALES MANAGER'S JOB

Results Desired	Job Specs
a. Reduce cost of selling by 5 per cent and overhead personnel costs by 15 per cent.	a. Knowledge of sales indexes and proven ability to recruit new good salesmen.

b. Expedite retirement of 10 per cent (5) of superannuated men; and recruit 20 per cent (10) new trainees the first year and 5 per cent (5) each year thereafter.

And so on . . .

b. Toughness required for either getting low producers to produce more, or retire or transfer them.

c. Inspiring appearance and manner; ability to make men want to work for him and his company.

And so on. . .

A special advantage to this approach is that you can develop charts like the foregoing and project them on a screen so that all the concerned persons—personnel manager, operating managers, the man's future boss, peers, and subordinates—can see, first, what results to expect of him; and secondly, what attitude, knowledge, skills, and ways of operating to expect of the man. The best man in the world will have a hard time getting results if the people who are supposed to cooperate with him keep thinking he ought to be doing something other than what he is doing. Also, it helps if you and others put priorities on the qualities you expect the man to have.

Bluntly stated, when the high-priority results are those requiring a get-tough policy, it's silly for people to try to find a "friendly, easy-going" man. Or, if change is needed, picking "safe old Sam," is obviously an error. And, if Department X is one that should maintain a highly repetitive, highly accurate type of work, then you don't want to send Young Turk McGill the Innovator into it, just because he's due for a promotion, and the boss job in Department X is suddenly vacant.

Sounds obvious, but until you chart the results against the job specs, you will find that people will have all sorts of contradictory expectations and will recommend men for jobs on the basis of the man's general ability and not upon the precise results to be expected.

Match the qualifications of the available men against the job

With the job specs in hand you can begin the process of matching the available candidates against the requirements of the job. Be sure to keep the priority of results and of job specs in mind, otherwise you may select a man for certain "halo" qualities or personality characteristics that you like, instead of for the things he ought to be able to do.

Here's where concentration on *forecasting* really pays off. When you hire someone or select someone for a job, you are in essence predicting what he will do. All right, keep predicting! That is, don't let yourself or others think, "Joe's a good guy, and he did a swell job for us in Cleveland. Let's reward him with this job." Instead, keep trying to visualize what the man will do in the job next year, five years from now, and how you can prove that he will live up to the forecast.

Again, a charting approach can help you compare a number of potential candidates against each other and against the job specs. Above all, be sure to establish the priorities of results, specs, and qualifications; then compare the candidates according to these priorities. Page 75 shows a comparison chart before the priorities have been decided.

As you develop these charts, or something like them, you can make the "trade-offs." Remember, too, the *time*

*Checklist for Matching the Qualifications
Against the Job*

Results Desired	Job Spec	Qualifications	Mr. A	Mr. B	Mr. C
Speed standard production	Production know-how / Drive	Electronic assembly production management experience	In 10 years in last job doubled production	—	Was assistant for 3 years in one of best production units in competitor's plant
Reduce costs	Cost control know-how / Persistence	Methods and time study training	While on loan in ZTZ plant cut costs 18%	—	—
Speed special orders	Production know-how / Drive	Production control background	—	Was head of production control unit	Some shop control experience
Improve materials handling	Know-how human relations	Conveyor, supervisory, and innovating experience	—	—	Has degree in materials handling

dimension. Are you hiring the man for one year, five years, or twenty years? Is the high priority item of today the one that will stay with you for many years, or is it just temporary? That is, don't allow a temporarily critical requirement to cause you to go overboard in hiring the "man that's got what we want."

For example, the company has had some bad breakdowns in the production control office just when the factory superintendent's position becomes open. Should you give priority to the man who has a reputation for being a production control expert? Yes, if production control is going to be the major problem for the next five years. But, no, if it is a temporary condition that can easily be fixed and the major problems are those involving the training of personnel in new products and processes, the handling of labor problems, and so forth.

Guarantee your forecast with a back-up plan

A fortuneteller or a radio commentator can sit back and wait for his predictions to come true (and boast about them) or not come true (and pretend he never made them). But a business executive has the responsibility to do what he can to make his forecasts work out successfully in practice.

If all our employees were supermen, our predictions would be infallible. But we must deal with men and women who have many defects and who run into personal problems—health, family, financial—that bring with them many "failure-factors" to upset our predictions.

A back-up plan, in essence, lists a man's deficiencies and

the steps that are being taken or will be taken to make up for them. For example, Mr. Jones has just been selected to be your new sales manager. One of the results you want him to achieve is a better equalization of territories, which of course means developing new market potential indexes and then persuading the salesmen to accept them. However, Mr. Jones has had no experience with such indexes. Obviously you have three choices: (1) Hire an assistant or consultant to help him; (2) Arrange for him to receive training in the preparation and use of such indexes; or (3) Give up your hope of achieving the equalization as long as Mr. Jones is sales manager.

Sounds obvious? Yet, you'll meet the situation again and again where a man is suddenly criticized for not having done something—something he didn't know how to do or didn't even know he was supposed to do. People all too often think that by giving a man a job, they automatically cause him to learn all about it. A back-up plan ensures that the man obtains the qualifications needed to achieve the desired results. Note how the following sample excerpt blueprints a practical approach to a successful future:

RESULTS DESIRED: Reduce handling costs in machine shop by $500,000.

MR. BROWN'S QUALIFICATIONS:
Adequate—Yes, in leadership of men and willingness to innovate.

Inadequate—Lacks knowledge of operations research, linear programming, queueing, and equipment costing.

BACK-UP PLAN: Arrange for after-hours courses at local

schools for him to learn enough to understand what must be done and to translate them to the men. Hire a technical expert to develop formulas, compute costs, depreciations, etc.

Three Blocks to Successful Personnel Forecasting

Overdependence on wishful hoping

The wishful or hopeful type of predicting consists in deciding the results you want and then wishing and hoping the man you select will be able to achieve them.

"I thought he'd make out all right," is often the signal that wishes have been substituted for careful analysis of qualifications and for a back-up plan. Only the person speaking should say, "I hoped," or "I wished," not "I thought."

Test your next prediction of a man's success by seeing if you can substitute the verbs "wish" or "hope" for "plan," "program," and "make sure." If it can be as easily said that you are wishing and hoping, then stop and start over. See what you and he can do to *ensure he can and will do what you predict for him.*

Overdependence on autocracy

If Mr. Al Wisher confuses his hopes with his predictions, Mr. Don Bossey, the autocrat, confuses his predictions with his commands. When wishing won't make things so, he demands that they become so. His expectations of his people are not based on an analysis of their past performance, skills, and interests. They are only based on his own determination. He asserts, I *must* have these sales quotas this year."

When Don Bossey fails to achieve results, he angrily concludes, "People won't work any more. I am going to have to get men who can do the job." But when he does hire a new man, his hiring decision is guesswork without facts. If the new man fails, out he goes, too. This wastes the time of both Bossey and his employees, but people are of little consequence to this autocrat. He is like a general who expends wave after wave of troops rather than change a faulty military plan.

Overdependence on policy

On the other hand, Mr. Percy Book relies too much on "policy." "In the past," he says, "we found that our Texas customers do not want shipments of our equipment during the summer." (This may have been true before air conditioning, but now the Texans are interested in year-round shipments.)

Policy is a partial guide to the future because it is based on past experience and often on too few facts. For example, you observe that when you shorten the coffee break, Sara works harder; but when you lengthen it, Mary Lou works harder. One manager observes only Sara and builds his policy on her; another observes Mary Lou and builds his policy on her production record.

Be on your guard about "nevers" like these:

Never send a non-college graduate to call on the medical trade.

Never let a woman represent you in a business dealing.

Never hire a man who has just been fired from another company.

Never hire a man who has ever worked for your competitor.

Never promote a man until he has been with the company for two years.

The foregoing show the marks of bureaucratic thinking, and too many of them indicate that it's not rigor in your thinking, but rigor mortis.

In brief, three types of executives who have low "prediction quotients" are:

TYPE	CHARACTERISTICS
1. *Wishful Thinker*	Hopes people will do what is appropriate.
2. *Autocrat*	Commands people to produce the results.
3. *Bureaucrat*	Expects policies to solve all human problems and to lead people to achieve results.

To Sum Up

Forecasting what people will do is particularly important because all the results we plan for must be achieved by people—the people we select, train, and back up.

Perhaps the biggest block to improving one's ability to predict what people will do is the lack of courage to go ahead and make the predictions. Once this obstacle is passed, you should decide the things you can control and those you can't control. With these in mind, you decide what *results* you want to achieve; what *work* or *job specs* must be employed to gain the results; what *qualifications* the holder of the job ought to have; which *applicant* has the optimum combination of qualifications; and finally, what steps to take to *back up* his success in the job.

In essence, the art of successful personnel predictions is based on three "probability factors," each of which is worth more than most people—and particularly the autocrat, bureaucrat, or wisher—can imagine. These are:

The "Probability Factor"	Share of the Odds
• Your own ability—try and you'll find you can make good, then better, and finally, reasonably valid predictions.	33%
• Analysis—of results desired and the job specs and applicant qualifications required.	33%
• Planned, continued efforts, with back-up from training, guidance, checks, and special assistance.	33%
• *The "luck factor"*	1%
	100%

how to

Use All Your Brainpower
in Making Decisions

SCIENTISTS SAY WE RARELY USE MORE THAN A fraction of our brainpower. We have millions of brain cells—the "thinking batteries"—and billions of combinations, or cell-assemblies. Yet, we use only a few thousand of these cells in a few millions of combinations. Smart people learn how to employ more of this unused capacity.

In business the real edge over competition and over costs lies in your brainpower and in that of the people working with you.

Think about that! In most industries you'll have the same wage rates as your competitor. You will buy materials at the same prices. Your equipment and buildings will cost you the same. Your advertising will cost you the same per line of exposure. What do you have that is different? Obviously, only your total brainpower; yet your competition has the same physical anatomy you do—the same number of human brain cells. The difference will be in how you *employ* yours.

The most important thinking you do is about people. What will *people* buy? To which *people* should you advance credit? Which salesman should be in charge of eastern sales?

**Faults That Lead to Poor
Decisions**

Poor decision-making usually involves one or more of the following faults:

1. Desire to have the decision make itself; that is, you just hope for the answer to "pop into" your mind.
2. Failure to obtain the facts needed about people, resources, money, time.
3. Failure to use the facts that you have.
4. Overemphasis on logic—you never give a creative hunch the chance to see the light of day.

Just as an athlete follows systematic procedures to ensure that his muscles are warmed up and that he puts everything into a shot, so does a mental athlete follow systematic steps to ensure that he puts all his thinking-power, both logical and creative, into each decision about people. This chapter will give you a systematic approach that will help you avoid the extremes of too much or too little logic in thinking about people.

**Steps in Making a Decision
About a Person**

Let's assume you have checked a move thoroughly from the technical business standpoint and from the organizational standpoint, and you are ready to make a decision about a particular human being. What are the steps and in what order should they be taken? Here they are—but watch out!

They sound deceptively simple:

1. Obtain the facts
2. Analyze the facts
3. Forecast the results
4. Make the decision

Facts first, decisions later

It's amazing how so many men "spin off" a decision first and later assemble facts to bolster it. Let's talk first about the facts you can observe yourself and then about the facts you gather through the eyes of other people.

GET—AND THEN USE—YOUR FACTS. Dan Olsen is a 44-year-old, seasoned plant executive who has been in charge of a losing operation for the past year in New Jersey. He was sent there with the full knowledge (of the Division Head, of Dan, and of everyone else concerned) that conditions in that area were such that the best any plant executive could do was to hold costs down and keep a toehold in the area. No one forecasts a profit for New Jersey.

At the end of the year, the company has an offer for the New Jersey plant. It decides to sell. But what to do with Dan?

First, what is Dan's value to the company? There is an economy mood in the top councils, and the suggestion is made that the company give Dan several months in which to locate himself with another company. After all, they say, he is only 44, and ought to find something. The suggestion is made by people who have complained about Dan before. The "anti-Dan" faction has on other occasions said:

Dan lacks enthusiasm and aggressiveness.
Dan doesn't look like a plant manager.
Dan lacks confidence.

The anti-Dan faction also emphasizes that Dan *might* have done better at the New Jersey plant.

It is a fact that Dan's plant lost money last year, but is it a fact that he—or someone else—should have done better? No, that is not a fact; that is an *opinion.*

SECONDHAND FACTS. The larger the company, the more often an executive must rely on facts brought him by other people. Therefore, you should teach people to bring you facts you can use.

In Dan Olsen's case, what were the facts about his performance as Plant Manager? From the Division Head's office, New Jersey is not so far that he need be content with knowing only Dan's gross profit or loss.

This company's performance review program held each plant manager accountable for results in these ten areas of the business:

1. Profits
2. Sales and Service
3. Product Quality
4. Manufacturing Costs
5. Industrial Relations
6. Accounting
7. Compliance with the law
8. Community Relations
9. Equipment Maintenance
10. Protection of Property and Assets

In its Plant Manager's manual, following the procedures recommended by some authorities*, each of these areas was

---

* SEE Walter R. Mahler and Guyot Frazier, "Appraisal of Executive Performance," in *Personnel,* March, 1955; and M. S. Kellogg, "Appraising the Performance of Management Personnel," *Personnel,* March, 1955.

spelled out in terms of at least three measures. For example, the manager was considered to have done a good job of managing product quality when no more than five complaints a year were received on any one product; when all major engineering specifications were met; and when impartial marketing surveys showed that the product reputation was unexcelled by any competitor.

Each of the ten areas was appraised twice a year (or more often) by outside inspectors. Thus, the Division Head had received quite a few objective reports of how well Dan was managing the plant. These reports added up to the following picture:

1.	Profits	POOR
2.	Sales	POOR
3.	Product Quality	EXCELLENT
4.	Manufacturing Costs	GOOD
5.	Industrial Relations	EXCELLENT
6.	Accounting	GOOD
7.	Compliance with Law	GOOD
8.	Community Relations	EXCELLENT
9.	Equipment Maintenance	GOOD
10.	Protection of Assets	EXCELLENT

These are secondhand reports, but they add up to a consistent picture of good management in many areas of plant operation. When the Division Manager showed this table of conclusions to his fellow executives (including some of Dan's severe critics), these men were impressed. These ratings were secondhand facts as far as the Division Head was concerned, but they were based on careful, firsthand observations of on-the-site facts. Dan was given a "fair shake." No more did the office politicians pass around vague remarks like

> Dan just doesn't look like a manager.
> He lacks confidence.
> He lacks aggressiveness and enthusiasm.

Now they could look back on the record and see what *results* Dan had gotten.

Nor was the report a whitewash. The low ratings on profits and sales were frankly discussed. The conclusion was that Dan had managed almost every aspect of the operation within his control and should be given a second chance.

Insist on analysis

One of the best executives we know used himself as a "blocking dummy" in most of his key conferences with his men. That is, he insisted they state their ideas first and try to knock his out of the way. He deliberately objected to the main points of their discussion. This forced them to think harder. It forced them to dig deeper into the real meanings of facts.

In the case of Dan Olsen, such an executive would not accept the common opinion that "Dan lacks enthusiasm and aggressiveness; he doesn't look like a plant manager; he lacks confidence." He would say to his men (and Dan Olsen's Division Manager actually did say this): "How do you *know* these things?"

Even after Olsen's Division Manager got the other executives to look at Olsen's record in terms of the duties of plant managers, the record still did not "speak for itself."

Why were profits down? *Why* were sales down? Did Olsen do *enough* to improve product quality and lower his costs?

It is a common fallacy that facts speak for themselves. They do not. Only managers can reach conclusions; only people can analyze what the facts mean. Insist on analysis; insist on determining what the facts about a man's performance actually mean.

Look ahead to results

The basic question about Dan Olsen, or any other employee under discussion, is not how he performed in the past; it is always· *How will he perform in the future?*

Failure to ask this question lies at the base of many wrong-headed management decisions about people. This cannot be more clearly illustrated than in the case of so-called "performance review" programs.

Earlier in this chapter we referred you to the writings of Mahler, Guyot, and Kellogg on performance review. While much good work has been done along the lines they recommend, many companies are coming to recognize that the very term performance review, implies looking backward and not forward.

This means that in the annual review conference between a man and his boss, the serious danger is that they will merely haggle about what went wrong last year. They will not take enough time to talk about what really counts: what they are going to do next year to get better results.

True, it is useless to talk about next year's work unless we know clearly what went wrong (and what went right also) this past year. But in many companies, the annual performance review session is the most wasted two or three hours of the year, in the opinion of disgusted managers. This is because they spend 95 per cent of their time on "spilt milk" and only 5 per cent on the more positive, constructive planning phase of their session together.

The principle, then, is:

> *Always ask what a man can accomplish in the future, if given the proper opportunity and support.*

We can apply this principle to decisionmaking situations of several kinds:

1. the transfer, selection or promotion decision, as in the case of Dan Olsen
2. the annual performance review session
3. deciding whether to put a particular employee into training
4. deciding how to handle a disciplinary problem.

HOW TO LOOK AHEAD. There is no ironclad formula for forecasting human behavior which we can sum up in a few lines here. This whole book is actually about forecasting and predicting, and toward the end we will be able to pull together the numerous guidelines and principles. But here there is space for a few hints and suggestions.

Five Keys to Accurate Forecasting

1. Past performance is the best guide to the future if conditions remain the same; we recommend a conservative

view of the individual, even if he makes sharp resolutions for improvement.

2. The older he is, the more past performance is the best guide to the future.

3. The most reliable forecasts will be of those things under the person's control; discount your forecasts of those aspects of his job which are subject to severe outside influences.

4. Still more reliable forecasts will be of the man's personality—how he reacts to the job, how he works with people, etc.; that is, people tend to stay in character. But research shows that some parts of a man's personality or character are more reliable than others:

   a. The most reliable forecasts can be made of his interests—what he likes to do, where he likes to put his time.

   b. The second most reliable forecasts can be made of his ability to solve problems—his intelligence, information, ability to express himself.

   c. Probably least reliable are his feelings and emotions; these can be judged only if you maintain fairly close and consistent contact with a person— this is one reason why close supervision is sometimes necessary for morale.

5. The best forecasts are made on the basis of all the available information—the worst are those made on the basis of vague hunches based on a few facts.

There is the case of the executive who forecast the success of job candidates based on their actions at lunch. He would take them to lunch and observe how they sliced their dessert. For example, if they cut off the point of a wedge of pie first, this meant they were afraid to be aggressive. This pseudo-psychology belongs in the realm of tea-leaf readings and astrology.

These suggestions for forecasting make so much common sense that some executives do not believe they can work and look for more exotic or fancy methods of forecasting, such as astrology. Why not try what is simple and straightforward?

But while they may be simple, the principles are neglected by some executives because it is not cheap to follow them. Time costs money. It takes time to review the facts. How much easier to accept the recommendations of your subordinates at face value?

Remember the one per cent rule; devote time to a decision in proportion to the risk you have if it goes wrong. A candidate for salesman paid $10,000 a year should have at least $100 worth of time devoted to the final decision to hire him.

Here's another way to look at it. In the case of Dan Olsen, how much was at stake from a purely financial standpoint? This 44-year-old, seasoned plant manager had been with the company for 13 years and had earned a total of $175,000. You have bought yourself a package of experience there. How much would it cost to replace it?

Make the decision

In the end, no matter how thorough your analysis, there is a risk. You will have to accept the fact that exactness about human behavior seems to be impossible. Take the risk like a man and go ahead and make the decision. This is what managers are paid to do.

If you follow the recommendations of this chapter and of the others in this book, you can cut the odds against you. For example, we know a company which operated five plants employing a total of 1000 workers. In three of the plants employment was fairly stable, but in the other two turnover was extremely high. Filling the 400 jobs in those two plants each year were *700 different production workers.*

Now, it is commonly estimated that the replacement cost for even a semi-skilled worker is at least $500 (for out-of-pocket costs). Turnover in these two plants cost the company $500 $\times$ 700, or $350,000! We suggested to the two plant managers that they hire a specialist to get the costs down; because if he cut the turnover by a tenth, he would more than pay for his fee.

The main point is: hiring errors (hiring standards were very low) were made in over half the people hired. If that batting average were, say, 50 per cent, and could be improved to 60 per cent, there would be an absolute improvement of 10 per cent and a relative improvement of 20 per cent. Turnover from bad hiring practices would be cut by $70,000 a year. Even a modest improvement in decision-making can yield large dividends!

The situation is similar to the major league hitter; he can get a bonus if he goes from .250 to .330, even though this means an improvement of from one hit in *four* to one hit in *three.* It doesn't *sound* spectacular when you put it that way, but it is.

Five Rules for Creative Decision-Making About People

Many people think there are no rules for creative thinking. They say, "Once you make a rule, then there is no creative thinking." But that in itself is a rule; in fact, disciplined, systematic approaches and methods are consistent with creative thinking. (But they must also encourage creative thinking.) Here are five rules for creative decision-making about people:

1. Creative decision-making must be based on an imaginative analysis of what a man can probably do in the future, not on a blame-centered analysis of what he has done in the past.
2. However, the best forecasts of what a man can do in the future require some knowledge of what he has done in the past.
3. Good decisions don't just happen without data—they should be built on facts.
4. Facts do not analyze themselves; it takes a hard-thinking, imaginative manager to figure out what facts mean.
5. Creative hunches based on a consideration of many solid facts—these are the basis of good forecasting; these are the output of your built-in, subconscious computer.

Five Guides for Mobilizing Executive Brainpower

You must do far more than learn this system of creative thinking yourself. You depend on other people—get them into the act also. Here are five suggestions:

1. Set up a regular procedure for reviewing the performance of people so that you get a factual report from objective inspectors, and not a hunch report from biased people.
2. Discourage the reporting of vague impressions with no factual basis by asking, whenever a rumor or impression is reported to you, *How do you know?*
3. When facts about performance are reported to you, insist on a searching analysis of *why* the facts are the way they are.
4. Encourage every conference about employees to work toward answering the question, "How will he perform in the future?" Discourage mere blame-fixing for the past.
5. Encourage your subordinates to seek even a slight improvement in their batting average on forecasting—remember, even a slight improvement (as in turnover reduction or in major league hitting) can have enormous positive consequences!

To Sum Up

The brainpower of yourself and of your subordinates is ultimately the only real edge you can maintain over your competition. Start today to cultivate it. Start to cultivate the maximum use of your capacity in applying to it decisions about human beings—your greatest business resource!

how to

Use the Decision
Programing Cycle

A GOOD BUSINESS, OPERATING EFFICIENTLY IN A common-sense way, is a pleasant thing to watch and a wonderful place in which to work. It's like a well-made electric clock; you know it's working, but you don't hear any noise.

Can "people problems" be handled quietly, simply? We do not claim that human problems are easy; but, as Kettering used to say, "The answer when found will be simple." We add: *If the answer isn't simple, look again.*

The DPC

All work is done in cycles: you set objectives, delegate the work, and return later to check it. You repeat this cycle over and over throughout your business year. As the wheel turns, work gets done; the business handles its affairs and, we hope, prospers.

The cycle we are most interested in here is the wheel of personnel decision-making. To emphasize its fundamental nature, let's call it the *DPC*, the "decision programing cycle."

The Three Spokes of the DPC

The first spoke of the DPC is the observation you make of the people at work. This information provides the initial impetus to turn the wheel, and it can be considered the "input" to the whole cycle.

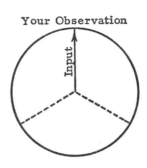

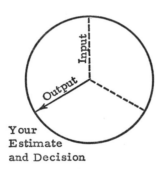

What is the "output"—the end result of the operation of this cycle? To jump to the last part of the cycle, we find that spoke is the output, the estimate you make of what the facts mean.

Between the first and the last spokes of the wheel, stands the second, the "analysis" of the facts or the observations. The complete turn of the wheel, then, consists of:

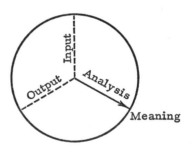

1. Observation of the facts
2. Analysis of the facts
3. Estimate of what is going to happen

The fundamental fact about the DPC is that it keeps turning. For example, after you make an estimate or decision (the last spoke of the wheel), the cycle shows you that another observation will be turning up. What does that mean? It means you should expect and look for feedback as to the accuracy of your estimate. The feedback brings the next wave of facts for you to analyze. You then make a new estimate of the situation. Neglecting any part of this cycle or trying to block any part of it will always cause trouble. Let's see why.

Observation of Performance

Whom should you observe? Too many men keep their span of observation all too narrow. Because you are in charge of one group of people doesn't mean you watch only them. You need to know about not just your immediate subordinates, but also other department heads, your superiors, your customers, and your suppliers.

The idea, for example, of "appraising" the performance of customers may strike you as novel. Yet, the key factors in any decision are the customers who may be affected. Too often, customers are neglected by businesses that are becoming more bureaucratic. Many a company has realized belatedly that the things they have done for "inside" personnel convenience have caused them to lose touch with "outside personnel," the customers.

Terence de Grazia, a supplier of fine wines, proudly served the best restaurant in town for 15 years. He took their account for granted and was undisturbed when they failed to pay their bills for as long as two months. The supplier, by not observing the restaurant's actual operation, failed to ob-serve that:

1. The building had not been repainted at the usual re-painting time.
2. Part of the restaurant parking lot had recently been sold.
3. New and rather frantic "cut-price" advertisements for cheap meals were now being run in the newspapers—something the "best restaurant" doesn't do.

You've guessed it. Times, neighborhood, and customers had changed, and after several years of struggle and chang-ing owners, the restaurant went bankrupt. Mr. de Grazia got stuck with the unpaid bills.

Horace Long: A Case of Non-Feedback

Horace Long, a 45-year-old specialist in computers, was hired by the Miller Manufacturing Company as a trouble-shooter for computer operators in the company's 15 plants. Long, permitted to operate on his own, planned his travel and accounted for his time to no one. The general managers of the plants never knew when he would appear on the scene, nor did the computer personnel.

Each plant manager thought no one wanted a report on Horace Long, so no complaints were made to the home office. When the computer personnel complained to their managers, the managers dealt with Long in their own ways. One man-ager told Long to stay out of his plant. Others hinted to him to stop barging into the plant and trying "to take over" computer operations without first clearing with the managers. Long did not report these run-ins to the home office.

After plenty of damage had been done, the following incidents came to light:

1. Long had countermanded instructions given by the general managers to their computer operators, and without notifying the general managers.
2. He had hired programmers for plants without getting the approval of their personnel departments.
3. He had used his home office connection to "lord it over" people.

Yet, all the management and technical reports had been indicating that the computer system was functioning; in other words, Long was getting the job done! Unfortunately, these reports did not include the harm being done to the morale among computer personnel and to the reputation of the "home office" for "backing" Long.

How do you prevent such a "rhubarb" from happening? Let's summarize the preventive methods under the following six headings:

Six Ways to Sharpen Your Observations

1. *Take frequent soundings during the early stages.* This applies not only to subordinates but also to new customers or a new boss.

2. *Accompany the person and collect direct observations.* Don't send a new man out alone. If you are too busy, send a trusted man out with him. Help him build his authority through that association, rather than through trying to "pull his rank" in other ways. And periodically, the same applies to an old-timer.

3. *Keep the door open for written or oral reports.* Watch for the silences or non-reports as well as the storm signals that appear in conversation and letters; these give hints long before the official reports come in.

4. *Follow up storm warnings as soon as you get them.* Don't wait for the roof to fall in or the tornado to arrive. Like icebergs, people tend to keep the big problems beneath the surface.

5. *It is false kindness to allow a person more freedom than he is mature enough to use properly.* Horace Long's personal weaknesses were abetted, not compensated for, by an inadequate system of performance observation.

6. *Technical qualifications should never be given such overriding importance that ordinary administrative prudence is overlooked.*

How to Make Sense of What You See

Everything we see in a man's performance can tell us about his ability or his motivation or both. Human ability means what a man knows, how well he can think, what he can do in working with people. Motivation means his interests and goals—what a man wants, what interests him, what he values. Every selling, supervisory, negotiating, and coordinating decision provides, as well as requires, an appraisal of other people's abilities and motivations.

> *Learn, therefore, to ask about every fact you observe about a person: "What does this fact tell me about his abilities? What does it tell me about his motivations?"*

The simplicity of the principles (observe, analyze, estimate) listed in this chapter leads even seasoned managers to believe they do them all constantly. In the same way, some men forget the necessity of careful records because they take them for granted.

The fundamental principle, then, is to:

> *Discipline your organization (and yourself) to ask for periodic reports on every employee (not necessarily in writing); ask each of your men for a report on each of their men:*
> a. *How is each man performing?*
> b. *What do the performance facts mean? That is, what do they tell you about the abilities and motivations of the people?*
> c. *What can and should be done?*

Most business troubles come from an omission of a fundamental practice. Hence, the need for insistent repetition by the head of a department or the head of a business upon the DPC of good judgment: Observe—analyze—estimate—feedback.

how to

Know When <u>Not</u> to

Make a Decision

THE MAN ON THE STREET PICTURES THE EXECUTIVE as sitting at a polished mahogany desk ten feet square, holding two phones with a beautiful blonde secretary standing by with a third long-distance call. To complete the picture, two underlings approach the big executive—"J. B.," they say, "this is the third week that our Upper Michigan plant has been in the red. What shall we do?"

J. B. takes his cigar out of his mouth, puts his hand over the mouthpiece of the telephone, and grunts, "Sell it."

A ridiculous picture of an executive? Yes, but to some extent, there is a little J. B. in all of us; we think we are really working when we are snapping out decisions. But a J. B. earns his salary by *both* the wise decisions he makes and the bad decisions he refuses to make or holds in abeyance. A J. B. earns his salary by knowing when to stall as well as when to move quickly.

Don't Let Others Force
Your Decision

The XYZ Corporation had expanded until it was on *Fortune* magazine's list of the top 500 companies in the

United States—and it was still growing. To fill out its lines of supply in a certain area, the XYZ Corporation wanted to buy the ABC chemical factory and invited the management of the ABC Company to a meeting to discuss the price.

The XYZ Corporation executives figured that the chemical company had a net worth of about $7 million, but that because of its special position in relation to their own corporation they would go as high as $10 million for it; however, they hoped to buy it for less than that.

The executives of the ABC Chemical Company arrived for the meeting in a seller's-market mood; they knew they were being courted; they were prepared to give all offers the hard eye. What happened? Let's tell it in the words of one of the participants, a young vice-president of the XYZ Corporation:

> We had, we thought, all our ducks in a row and were all set to finish up the negotiations in a business-like fashion within a day or so. It did appear to me that the ABC people were only half-interested, and the odds of a complete turn-down from them were fifty-fifty. When we all got together our President Mr. Jones started talking, and to my horror and embarrassment, he began a long, rambling disquisition on *our* corporation. I thought, "Ouch! The old boy has gone senile!" He rambled on about the good old days when he was building up the XYZ Corporation. Instead of asking questions about the ABC Company or discussing possible terms, Mr. Jones boasted about the size, complexity, operations, and products of his own company. He kept this up for three days! Those of us who worked under him, of course, couldn't speak up. We sat and suffered. The representatives from the ABC Company

also got restless, but every time one of them started to talk about the ABC Company, Mr. Jones would interrupt with something like: "That reminds me, do you know our corporation has over a hundred million in assets in foreign countries?" Or, "Last year our sales of our new fibers were 20 per cent over our competitors." And so on.

Well, what happened? By the end of the third day the representatives from the ABC Company, instead of sitting back waiting for the XYZ to make a proposition, had become almost frantic to get something done. Suddenly one of them blurted out: "Say, how about setting a price on our company?"

Now Mr. Jones allowed himself to be persuaded to talk terms. In the end, the XYZ Corporation bought the ABC Company for exactly $7 million! And the next day, Mr. Jones was back to his crisp, decisive self. He had stalled all of us by talking about *his* company, rather than about the *other* man's company and had built a reverse pressure against our willingness to pay the other's high price.

In short: Don't make decisions at a pace set by others. Mr. Jones didn't.

Check Both Hot and
Cold Reactions

The ancient Persians when faced with a tough decision would make it once while sober and again while drunk. The ancient Greeks would sleep on it or fast for 24 hours. What do these practices ensure? They ensure that you consider a matter while you are in one mood and again while you are in another.

Making decisions about people necessarily involves many intangibles and many emotional reactions. We are all a bit "manic-depressive," which means we have our ups and downs. A good decision is one that we can implement—or live with—whether we are feeling dynamic or tired and depressed. A man that fits well with our cheerful, aggressive moods may disappoint us when we are tired and want him to be a self-starter, not a follower. Therefore, always try to take several observations of the other person (and of yourself). Do this over an adequate period of time. Plotting this approach as a matrix can help you check that you have done so. (See the diagram on page 109.)

Check Your Hunches

Freud once said that in unimportant decisions, be very technical in weighing pros and cons; but in vital matters, follow your hunches. What he meant, of course, by a vital matter is something like marriage, choice of career, way of life, etc. These are things *you have to live with;* and, therefore, cost-effectiveness, efficiency, prices, depreciation, bargains, and so forth are not the important factors. How you will *feel,* how you will enjoy yourself, or suffer, or be proud, or regret—all these are what count. These come from deep inside yourself.

Therefore, before you make a decision look at it with this question in mind: "Is this a technical matter, or is it something that will affect my way of life, my emotions, my satisfaction?"

His Attitude (Timing)

Your Attitude (Timing)	Early A.M.	Late P.M.	Early in week	End of week	When he's on the up	When he's on the down
Early morning						
Late afternoon						
First of week						
End of week						
When things are going well						
When things are going badly						

Check your impressions in the appropriate boxes; and at the end of a week or so, you can see how you and he match your up and down slopes of energy, enterprise, and effectiveness. Ideally, impressions should be well-scattered and not always in the same boxes.

If it is a technical matter, then the only reason for delaying will be to make sure you have all the costs and legal or procedural details taken care of. Check them off like a pilot running through his pre-takeoff flight plan.

If the matter will affect your life, then stop and get by yourself long enough to visualize how things will be in the future, depending upon your decision. Go about it the way a woman picks the colors for her livingroom. If she has lots of money, she can experiment. If she doesn't, she knows that whatever she buys she'll have to enjoy or suffer with for a long time.

Most personnel decisions involve emotions and personality; before making a personnel decision, be sure to check your "instinct" and that of others who will also be affected.

Start the Investigation About
Any Uncertain Facts

Fred Inglish had headed up the Jones Company's Customer Service Department for six years. Fred, an idea man, was well-liked, though extremely ambitious.

Mr. Jones, the President, wanted to replace the sales manager but could not find anyone in the Sales Department who could do the job. Fred Inglish seemed the best choice because of his ideas, drive, and intelligence. However, he had not been tested in a line position, leadership, nor in getting results as a salesman. Accordingly, the other executives warned Mr. Jones to test Fred in an assistant's job before making him sales manager. Mr. Jones believed that: "The minute I make Fred Inglish assistant sales manager, the cat is out of the bag as to what I am thinking, and there will be trouble. We will have to promote Fred without the trial period you mention."

Fred Inglish was promoted, and then made nearly every mistake in the book before he learned how to supervise the salesmen.

Obviously, Mr. Jones should have delayed the *action* if not the *decision* to promote Fred Inglish. Too often, people equate action and decision, and need and fulfillment. Mr. Jones was right in seeing that the sales manager ought to be replaced. Perhaps, too, conditions required immediate action, and Fred Inglish was the best available. But giving him the title did not give him the skills and knowledge he needed. Accordingly, the President and other executives should not have stopped with the "fait accompli"—the finished fact of the promotion—*but they should have continued to investigate what Fred Inglish needed in the way of experience, training, and help.* They should have done *after* his promotion what they would have done before it, had there been time enough!

The vice-president in charge of the Havoil Company's foreign operations was asked to decide George Feather's suitability for duty in a foreign area (where the company's practice was to send no one over 35 because the work was hazardous and demanding). George Feather's written background made a good case for his selection. He was intelligent, genuinely interested in the move, and had good recommendations. Some aspects of George's resume appeared incomplete or fuzzy, but the vice-president couldn't put his finger on just what was "offbeat."

The V-P checked with several former employers of George Feather. Each had the same type of reaction: "Yes,

George did a good job. No, it is difficult to make an unqualified recommendation—exactly why, I can't say." The V-P's inquiries produced quite a dossier of information about George—and more confusion. But the deadline for the move came; and George got the assignment because the V-P felt a move had to be made, and he couldn't state any explicit objections.

But six months later, George's clearance for access to some government contract matters was denied by the government representative. At the same time, the personnel officer of the overseas unit questioned George's integrity because of some serious incidents with which he had been involved overseas.

The V-P reinstituted inquiries into George's background, and now people really checked into the inconsistencies. For instance, George had claimed to be 35 (in 1963). Yet, he had a Purple Heart from a foot wound in Guadalcanal. How could he be 35 in 1963, and have fought in Guadalcanal in 1942? This "trivial question" turned up some interesting information. George, 41 in 1963, had been lying about his age for years. He had always tried to appear younger than he was. Lying had become a habit, and no one knew how much of George's word to rely upon. But it was clear that George had been the wrong choice for the job.

Again, the point is clear: Always make the investigation into a man's reference and background that is justified by the importance of the position—even though you have to make the investigation *after* he has obtained the job. Having to make a decision in a hurry doesn't relieve you of the responsibility for establishing its soundness, particularly when human beings are involved.

Establish Your Times
of Decision

You know how the Supreme Court and certain other courts have their "decision dates"—the date on which they announce their decisions in various cases. Among the advantages of this practice are: it reduces speculation; it keeps people from hounding the judges; and lets people know when to expect the decision, one way or the other. Why not apply the practice to your own decisions?

When you have a matter to decide, make an estimate of when the decision should be *announced*. You may actually make the decision much sooner, but you *don't* announce it until that date or hour.

How do you estimate the time of announcement? You simply balance the following factors and take the time that fits them optimally:

● THE DEADLINE: The time you must announce the decision so a hiring or firing date can be met, or a bill paid, or materials purchased, etc. Obviously, you must announce your decision by that time.

● THE KINDLY DATE: Suppose one or more people will have to "sweat out" your decision? If so, then in charity and decency, you want to tell them, other things being equal.

● THE FACTS-AND-THOUGHT DATE: Every decision requires the accumulation of pertinent facts and then the mulling over them. From experience, you should be able to predict how long this will take you.

● THE SECOND-THOUGHT PERIOD: In addition to the above, you want to allow as much time as possible for second-thoughts and for the "hot and cold" and "hunch" factors we have already discussed.

● THE SIDE-EFFECTS DATE: The speed with which you announce a decision has its side effects; that is, it either impresses people with your prompt decisiveness, or it disappoints them with your apparent casualness. If you are running late in a number of things, be quicker to announce your next few decisions. If you have been snapping out a number of decisions with short fuses, then be slow to announce the next few decisions. Above all, don't announce personnel decisions too quickly; people don't like to have their lives and affairs given short shrift. They want you to take a careful, considerate, *judicial* approach to whatever involves their standing in the business—pay, discipline, promotion, assignments, and so forth.

Once you have picked the date, then announce when you will make the decision. For example, "All right, I'll look into the matter, and let you know next Tuesday around 11 A.M." The specific time is reassuring; it gives both you and the other person a deadline, letting you deal with other things meanwhile; and it shows you are going to collect and sift the facts.

Suppose the decisions are trivial? If so, try to collect them in a bundle and announce them all at once. For example, "See me Friday afternoon around 3 P.M. My secretary is putting together a list of items like yours, and I want to look them all over at the same time. Then I can be sure I don't overlook any."

The key point: Distinguish between making a decision and announcing it. And don't be in too big a hurry to announce every decision as fast as you make it. It's nice to get them off your desk and to feel you are giving a display of great promptness; but ripeness, timing, and "judicial" effect are also important. Therefore, have the nerve and the patience to let certain decisions simmer a bit longer and to hold off announcing them as long as possible.

Try to Wait Until "It Feels Right"

We often can and ought to hold up a decision until the time is ripe for it. This takes courage because most of us feel uneasy and impatient when faced by a number of choices. As Bruce Barton put it: "Great men suffer hours of depression through introspection and self-doubt. That is why they are great. That is why you will find modesty and humility the characteristics of such men." Also, you will find they have the courage to tolerate temporary indecision and to stand firm amid pressures to "get the matter over with."

Among the "no-decision" signals are the following:

- The facts are not impressive—they don't point decisively toward the "right" decision.
- The decision to be made involves considerable risk—financial or personal.
- Something seems missing in the case.
- You have not mulled over the case.

- You can't get a focus on the man as a person; you can't visualize him and his reactions clearly.
- You don't feel right and natural about the decision that has been proposed.

Summary: The Rules for When Not to Decide

This chapter has sought to break the "prompt-decision" fixation that many of us have been persuaded to adopt over the years. Of course, we needn't go to the other extreme and become delayers and foot-draggers. What it does mean is that we keep the three distinctions in mind: the soundness and growth of the decision itself; outside pressures that may make us hasten it or delay it; and finally, the time for announcing it—which is something quite different than the time to arrive at the decision. Let's set up the following rules:

1. Don't let others force your decision—if so, they are working to their benefit, not yours.
2. Check your decision from hot and cold standpoints: See how it looks when you are rested and dynamic and when you are tired and depressed.
3. Check your hunches, instinct, or intuition when important decisions about people are required. If the hunch isn't right, don't make the decision.
4. If you must make a premature decision, don't stop your investigation of the facts. Continue to think and to explore as though you had not made the decision. This will:

    a. Protect you from otherwise unforeseen conse-
quences;

    b. Prepare you in the event you have to reverse the
decision;

    c. Keep any deficiencies or weaknesses in mind so that
you and others can continue to work on them.

5. Don't announce a decision just because you've gotten it
made: Pick the right time and place for the announcement; and until that time comes, you "have no comment."

how to

Avoid Stress in

Decision Making

A MOVIE MAGNATE, ASKED IF THE STRESS OF HIS work gave him ulcers, roared: "I don't get ulcers—I give 'em!"

There are all too many companies in which the concept of executive work includes getting, or giving, ulcers. This is an absurd situation, because men who work under constant stress cannot continue to do their best.

Dr. Hans Selye has made many experiments that demonstrate the effect of stress on animal and human organisms. For instance, he has demonstrated that rats subjected to heat, cold, hunger, and overcrowding, though not sick with any injury or infection, died sooner than rats not subjected to "pressures." One of his recent experiments appears most significant. He placed two identical groups of rabbits in two identical cages and provided them with the same food, air, water, and "animal comforts." One cage, however, was kept in a place where a dog could run around it and bark at the rabbits each day. At the end of six months, autopsies were performed on all the rabbits. Those that had undergone the daily "stress" from the dog had all the signs of premature coronary disease, including clogged arteries, while the other "calm" rabbits did not.

How many of us are wearing ourselves out under the illusion that we are paid to work under stress; that we have got to make it look that way or else others will think we are loafing? Yet, unless work can be handled in a "natural way," it means you are under stress. Too much stress is unhealthy and can ruin a complex decision, especially a complex decision about people.

Don't Be Grim About People

Grim men do not make good decisions about people, because grimness keeps a man from putting himself in the shoes of another. The extremely serious person is often too preoccupied with himself. He may be worried about his own ability to do his job. Or, he may not have grown up. Or, he may not be in the best of health. When we don't feel well, good humor is often the first thing we lose!

You will also find that an executive is too irritable or impatient to assemble the information and to do the calm thinking required for good personnel decisions.

Relax Yourself into the Other Person's Role

When two fishermen are talking about their catches, each describes the length of his prize fish, how long it fought him, and so on. They appear to be listening to each other, but each man is patiently waiting for the other to finish so he can tell his own story. They are relaxedly enjoying listening to themselves talk, and they don't really hear each other.

But suppose two men are negotiating the sale of a car. The salesman asks, "What kind of car are you looking for?" The buyer says, "I just want transportation—nothing fancy." The salesman replies, "I understand, Mr. Jones. Le'ts go out on the lot, and I will show you several which are tops for reliability, economy, and convenience."

In which of these conversations does the one man really try to put himself in the shoes of the other? Obviously, it is the auto salesman.

Men under stress, or preoccupied with their own difficulties, can not take the role of the other person. True, relaxation by itself does not automatically lead a man to put himself in the shoes of the other person. The fishermen were relaxed, but still not really listening to each other.

The auto salesman, however, by seeking to take the role of his customer, can be more relaxed and more effective than the high-pressure salesman who, listening only to his own desires and pressures, tries to sell what *he* wants to sell, and at his price.

Note the important distinction between relaxed listening for purely social purposes, and relaxed listening for the purposes of entering the buyer's mind in order to understand better how to deal with him. Again, a sense of pressure, stress, and nervous doubt is a signal that you are seeking only *your* side, and not that of the others who are involved. When you begin to feel and act grimly, the signal is reaching emergency-warning size.

Humor and Decision
Making

When business stops being fun, it is time to take stock of the situation and of yourself. There is a close connection between spontaneous, creative thinking (such as is needed for success in business) and humor. The basis of humor, like that of creative thinking, is the new twist given a relationship.

But not all "humor," nor all "creative thinking," leads to desirable ends, so let's review some distinctions.

DESTRUCTIVE VS. CONSTRUCTIVE HUMOR. Ridicule of a person is destructive, as when one destroys a man's reputation with a few sharp remarks. For example, many people believe that a major contributing factor to Dewey's loss of the presidency was the remark made about him by Dorothy Parker: "He looks like a little man on a wedding cake." Similarly, Willkie's chances were reduced by the biting effect of Harold Ickes' epithet: "Wendell Willkie, the barefoot boy from Wall Street."

On the other hand, constructive humor about a man can lead us to regard him with all the more affection, especially when the humor has made him more human, or has highlighted one of his good qualities.

For instance, we can pronounce the word *bureaucrat* with a contemptuous sneer, and add that they are "pigs feeding at the public trough." The same point was made about Washington bureaucrats, and more constructively, by Woodrow Wilson when he said, "Every man who takes office in Washington either grows or swells." This remark is humorous, and it leaves the door open for *some* bureaucrats becoming able and very human beings, even though others "swell like hogs."

Though Will Rogers' sly humor mercilessly revealed people's weaknesses, his jokes were never destructive of reputations worth preserving.

We all prefer to work for a man who is warm, human, and interesting. Why? Because we feel we will get a "fair shake" from him. Yet, there need be no incompatibility between this "ideal boss" and a determined, hard-driving boss. People with a warm sense of humor are not lacking in ambition; they just know when to relax and when NOT to take themselves too seriously. We all have some sense of humor when the joke is on someone else. A real sense of humor means the willingness to take a joke on ourselves.

Note the effortless swing of the professional ball-player. A Stan Musial, for instance, swings hard but not desperately. Arnold Palmer lets go with a powerhouse try at the ball—but it is controlled power.

Similarly, business decisions should be made with smooth, relaxed, concentrated power; not with a nervous, tense, desperate and irritable "chopping" at the ball.

Five Hints for Relaxing in Business

1. Stress is *unused energy*. Look to see how you can channel it constructively.

2. Don't be the man who frets over his work, stays awake half the night, calls up his subordinates to ask additional questions, and arrives tired the next morning. He may think he is applying great energy to his business problems, but in truth he is misapplying it.

3. Be ready to shift easily from one task to another. The narrow-gauge specialist becomes upset over variations; the *executive* learns to shift gears with a light, ready touch.

4. Organize your life to balance between work, play, rest and affection in accordance with the ancient rule "nothing too much."

5. Keep your sense of humor; and if you find yourself losing it, stop and rethink your way of life.

Stress vs. good decision

If a washing machine is not fastened to the floor securely, the rotation of the container will not be wholly consumed in washing the clothes, but will be partly dissipated in shaking the machine. The human mind is like a machine, in that improperly directed energy causes wasteful vibrations!

A basic principle, then:

> I. *The executive should recognize the signs of unused energy in himself and not let them be passed on harmfully to others.*

A tense executive will drive people away from him just at the time he needs their help. His manner will also engender in them stress and will disorganize their problem-solving abilities.

What to do about it? The remedies for stress basically boil down to (a) improved organization of effort, (b) changing activities when they prove stressful, and (c) cultivating a philosophy of management which prevents stress from accumulating beyond a certain point.

Organizing your effort

An executive will worry less about what his people *ought* to do, if he will think more about what they probably will and can do. This returns us to our discussion of the DPC cycle, which we reaffirm here as a principle:

> II. *Stress is reduced when executives cultivate the use of the DPC cycle; when they organize their thinking about people; collect facts in an orderly way; analyze these facts; and estimate what results they will probably get from various courses of action.*

Changing activities to avoid stress

Change of pace helps reduce stress. It acts like a valve in a steam boiler. But a "break" is useless if tense men continue the same argument. Nor is a lunch a change, when it is a business lunch. But not all of us need big changes. A shift in activities at the desk may be enough. For example, when an engineer can't solve a difficult problem in factory lay-out, he should put it away for a couple of hours and work on some other blueprints.

III. *Stress is reduced when a person changes what he is doing, redefines his task, or takes a fresh view of it.*

Developing a stress-easing philosophy

The right philosophy can help us look at stress more constructively. Stress is not going to go away because we don't like it. *We* are the ones who have to change!

If a lot of the fun has gone out of business, we suggest you take a new look at your philosophy of managing stress. Because, either you manage your stresses, or they will manage you!

The first thing to recognize in this connection is that work itself does not put stress on us. For example, people are not difficult; it is the way we look at those people which makes them *look* difficult. It's what happens inside us—not outside—that counts.

Look back on a job you had five years ago. Who was the most difficult person you had to work with? He (or she) doesn't look like such a foul ball now, does he? Our views of people mellow with time. Much of our difficulty with people is in our minds; and this is probably easier to change than to change the people. As a wise man once said: "The only things you should really fear are your own thoughts."

IV. *We can reduce stress by realizing that it is our image of another man that is often at fault. Change your image, and the other man seems less difficult.*

Of course, not all the people who are "no damn good" are just that way in your mind. But it starts there, and the mind's image of others causes much of the stress. But no matter how much you improve the image you have of a person, the fact can remain that he doesn't do what you want. This is a key source of stress: when things do not happen as you expect.

But here again, the constructive approach is not to stew over the failure, but to recognize the failure of people to do what you want as (a) an inevitable part of life, (b) an interesting part of life, and (c) requiring improved estimates on your part.

> V. Stress is reduced when we accept the fact that people will do what we expect only part of the time; when we look upon the unpredictability of other people as interesting, amusing, or instructive; and when we strive to estimate what people will do, rather than worrying about why they don't do what we think they ought to do.

Four Roads to Relaxation

Let's sum up this chapter by the following four roads, or ways, to relaxation:

1. Excess stress is unused energy and can disrupt the creative ability of the executive and of his people.

2. Unused energy is made usable when one organizes it by using orderly processes of decision-making.

3. A fresh view of your work and of yourself can reform your philosophy of stress. Recognize that it is you who puts yourself under stress, and not your job or "those other people."

4. Accept the fact that no one will do what you predict 100 per cent of the time; that this fact can make people interesting and even more entertaining to you. Estimate what another person is likely to do, not just what he ought to do.

how to

Develop and Use

3-D Curiosity

Questions About People

To expand your horizons of understanding, you must learn to ask the right questions about people. The right questions are those that can actually be answered; provide useful knowledge; and deepen your understanding, as well as solve immediate practical problems.

On the other hand, the wrong kinds of questions are those whose answers do not lead anywhere. For example, someone notices that Robert Jones, the Engineer, spends most of his time in his office. Someone asks, "Why doesn't Jones come out of his office? Is he an introvert or something?" This question gains nothing but trouble, whether the answer is Yes or No.

If we say, "Yes, Jones is an introvert," then many of us think that explains why a man stays in his office. Actually, it explains nothing at all. If we say, "No, Jones is not an introvert," then many of us think that means he is an "extrovert," and we accept that word as meaning that usually Jones likes to get out and mix with people. But the word *extrovert* explains almost nothing about Jones, and we fool ourselves by using it.

Answers Should Make a Man
an Individual

The questions you ask about people lead someplace if they produce answers which make an "individual" out of each person. What does that mean? It means questions like the following:

What does Bob Jones actually do or say?
What does he think his job is?
How does Bob feel about the company?
What is his relationship with his immediate superior?
What is his previous job history?
What is his education?
What is Bob trying to achieve in his career with this company?
What are his long-range hopes and plans?
What does Bob think about his own performance; his strengths and weaknesses?

Such questions probe into the patterns underlying Bob's conduct. Therefore, they provide information with which to "extrapolate" to his future conduct.

Look for the 3-D Questions

Note that the foregoing questions about Bob Jones can be divided into three groups.

DIMENSIONS	GROUPS	TYPICAL QUESTIONS
1. Present dimension	About his present job	What does he think his job is? What is he working on? What are his relationships with his immediate superior?

DIMENSIONS	GROUPS	TYPICAL QUESTIONS
2. Past dimension	About his previous career	What is his previous job history?
		What is his education?
3. Future dimension	About his future or anticipated career	What is Bob trying to achieve in this company?
		What are his long range hopes?
		What does he think of his own abilities and limitations?

All questions about a person pertain either to his present, past, or future. A well-rounded picture of a person requires all three "dimensions." The more such questions we ask about a man, the more of an individual he becomes in our eyes.

For example, suppose that in the case of Bob Jones we not only observe that he spends most of his time in his office, but also talk to his immediate superior and find that Bob has not been productive as an engineer. A 3-D picture of Bob will tell us why not, and what to do about it.

Probing into the past we find out that:

1. Bob's father was an outstanding automotive engineer.
2. Bob made only average grades in engineering school.
3. The only really successful job he has ever had in the

past was during two summers when he had a part-time job selling boats.

Talking to Bob about his concept of what he thinks his job is, we learn from him that:

> The company wants me to come up with some brilliant new designs for equipment. They can't forget that my father made a major contribution to the automatic gear shift, I guess.
>
> I have got to keep my nose to the grindstone until I come up with something. The last ten months I have been working on a transmission design and haven't come up with anything yet.

Further investigation shows that Bob would sincerely like to come up with some productive ideas, especially since his boss is a friend of his father, but that he is greatly discouraged and does not really think his talents lie in this direction. When asked what he would really like to do if he had his choice, Bob said, "Frankly, I would like to sell small power-boats."

Does this picture of the individual, Bob Jones, begin to come through, now? He probably sticks in his office (and doesn't circulate around among the other engineers as much as he really should, to pick up some ideas), not because he is an "introvert," but because he feels under pressure. Not only that, but he is not getting any place, knows it, and wants to do something else. By being curious about the man, Bob Jones, we have gotten into some really basic questions about his productivity and whole career.

Testing the Pattern

When you turn on the TV set, you automatically note:

Is the sound clear or garbled?
Is there a double image?
Is there enough contrast?
Is there rolling of the image?

If not, you turn the knobs to correct the problem.

By the same token, you should check not just for a good 2-D image but for a clear 3-D image of each man with whom you deal in everyday business life. Just as you test the TV pattern for sound, image, contrast, and rolling, you can test the 3-D pattern to be sure you have a true picture of the man as an individual.

In everyday business life there are probably 10 to 20 people who are most critical for your own success. They would include some of your large customers, your key subordinates, and two or three of the people over you in authority. You had better test the 3-D pattern you have of these people.

Ask yourself these "test questions":

Do I know how things are going for him and how he feels about his work?
Do I know something about the outside pressures (from his family and social life) to know why he operates in business the way he does?
Do I know enough about his past career to know why he operates in business the way he does?
Do I know what he is trying to accomplish in the future —what he is working toward?

Don't Make the "Birthday Mistake"

Obviously we are talking about far deeper knowledge of a man than just knowing his birthday, number of children he has, and if he is in good health.

An executive, advised by some "expert" to send each employee in his department a birthday card, did so faithfully for years—until he found out that the women over 35 did not like being reminded of their birthdays!

We are talking about knowing what an employee thinks of himself and his company; about understanding his hopes and fears; about the happy or bitter experiences that helped form him the way he is today. These questions are a lot more basic than birthdays.

How to Avoid Invading Privacy

Will all this recommended questioning constitute an invasion into a man's privacy? Not if it is done for the right reasons and in the right way. Listening in on people can be mere eavesdropping or prying, and talking about them can become barefaced gossip. The test is: Are you doing it for personal entertainment, or to enhance the business? Are you studying people in order to take advantage of them, or to help them accomplish their goals and those of the business?

Isn't the job the only important thing?

It is impossible to understand a man's performance just by watching it. All you can do is to know what he is doing, and perhaps how well. You can't know *why* he does what he does, or what might be done to help him change it. For example, if a man mistrusts his boss, the experience often dates back to earlier bosses who, in his eyes, let him down.

If an employee is apathetic and not putting out maximum effort, this poor performance usually does not make sense unless you talk to him and find out, for example, that the future seems an empty place, that he has no hope for a better life, and that he has given up doing more than the minimum. Why does he think these things? Until you can answer this question—which requires a 3-D picture—you can do relatively little to help him change.

A typist is not meeting her quota. The supervisor must ask "why not?" The answer must be based on more than merely observing *what* she is doing. A 3-D image will give a picture of job performance in depth, as it is, and how she sees it. In addition, it shows how it got to be that way and where the employee seems to be headed in her career—what she thinks she is working *for*.

The job *is* the important thing; but we don't ever really understand job performance unless we can see it *in depth*.

Who needs to know?

The real safeguard of each person's privacy is the organization itself. That is, the organization of a company says who works for whom. The person has to know his immediate subordinates, and they have to know him. Anyone else in on the conversation is eavesdropping, spying, or gossiping.

Notice that real gossips and rumor-mongers are rarely talking about people whom they have a *right* to know about.

The grapevine covers every subject in the world *except* what is legitimate. Gossips and rumor-mongers are not trying to understand other people in 3-D. They are merely complaining, criticizing, or evaluating without really having the facts.

Six Steps Toward 3-D Pictures of People

1. List the people around you for whom you do or do not have clear 3-D pictures. Adjust your focus accordingly.

2. *Don't* use questions which classify people into vague groups, such as:
   Is Jones introverted or extroverted?
   Is she a trouble-maker?
   Is the boss neurotic?
   Is Gwynn Roberts a mulatto?
   Is he Jewish?

3. *Do* ask questions that reveal a man's feelings about the job, his history and background, his hopes and plans for the future—questions that best point to the individual.
   If you have a bias (such as looking only at his past history and forgetting his present efforts), broaden your perspective.

4. Ask these questions at the right time and about the right people. Encourage others in your business to do the same thing.
   Discourage people in your business from rumor-mongering, gossip, and petty criticism. The best way to do this is to *encourage* them to concentrate on

understanding the people they are supposed to understand.

5. Check the image you have of your immediate subordinates, associates, and superior. Do you know how each person feels about what he is doing, some of his past experiences, and his outlook toward the future?

   You don't need to make a point of being nosy. Normal conversation is quite enough. Just find something about how people feel—that's quite enough to improve the image.

6. Take steps to make your image current, and to keep it that way. The people in your business are changing all the time. Any fixed image you have of these people will eventually get out of focus.

   Remember: The creative, curious man learns more about his business all the time. The curious man asks questions that lead to constructive answers. There isn't any other real road to success in business.

how to

Find Out Facts

About People

Facts vs. Fiction

It's always a shock to realize how few decisions in business are actually based on fact. For example, too many managers will accept vague opinions or feelings in lieu of factual information about a subordinate. Note the following case.

Glen Emmett was a seasoned merchandising man who had been recruited by the Electrocoil Company ostensibly for its Personnel Department, but in reality to set up a new Sales Training Department. The Personnel Department had the backing of the Electrocoil President for this plan, but did not clear it with the sales managers.

Naturally, Glen soon began to edge into personnel problems of the sales divisions as a step toward his eventual role as head of the Sales Training Department.

The sales heads became suspicious. "What's this guy trying to do?" one of them asked the Personnel Manager. "Last week he asked all my area sales offices to give a list of salesmen they had fired during the last two years."

The Personnel Manager, not wanting to appear to usurp the President's prerogatives, did not tell the sales division heads that training would eventually be taken out from under them. So, he had to answer in a lame, confused fashion.

Shortly thereafter, the President asked the key managers their opinions of Glen Emmett. They said:

> He's hard to talk to. People can't figure out what he is driving at half the time.
>
> He has been meddling in our division's operations.
>
> For the field Glen is in, he is one darn poor communicator.

The President called the Personnel Manager and told him that Glen Emmett was the wrong man for the proposed Sales Training Department.

What were the facts? The comments made by the sales division heads were not facts about Glen Emmett. They were facts about the feelings and attitudes experienced by *the division heads*. Let's restate the remarks in more objective terms:

ORIGINAL COMMENT	COMMENT RESTATED
Glen is hard to talk to.	I found Glen hard to talk to.
People can't figure out what he is driving at half the time.	I can't figure out what he is driving at half the time.
He has been meddling in our division's operations.	The other day, he asked my area sales managers for a list of the salesmen who had been fired the last two years. I resented this.

For the field Glen is in, he is one darn poor communicator.	With the experience I have had with him, I can't recommend him as a good communicator.

The comments on the right can provide the President with some *clues* about *what is going on*. He might see that at least part of the trouble lies in the vague assignment Glen has been given and in the secrecy about the proposed training department.

Suppose you were the President and wanted a *factual* picture of Glen Emmett. How would you go about it? Obviously you would ask probing questions like the following:

COMMENT RESTATED	PROBING QUESTIONS
I found Glen hard to talk to.	When did you talk to him? What were you talking about? Who else was there?
I can't figure out what he is driving at half the time.	When was the last time you had trouble figuring out what he was driving at? How did you happen to be talking to him?
The other day, he asked my sales managers for a list of salesmen, etc.	Tell me more about this survey he was making; didn't the personnel department clear it with you?

With the experience I have had with Glen, I can't recommend him as being a good communicator.	Give me some more examples. When, where, and how did you talk to him in each instance? Who else was there?

The questions in the right-hand column parallel those of a lawyer or journalist. They ask for *specifics*: *where something happened*; *what happened*; *who else was there as a witness*.

To test the "fact-ness" of a "reported fact," see if you can tell clearly:

- Who observed it
- Where it happened
- What happened to what, or to whom
- Who else was there

When such specifics are missing, you are not dealing with a fact, but with an opinion.

A Systematic Approach for Getting Facts

Too many businessmen do not know what is going on in their own business, because they have not systematized their way of producing facts. Basic to any system is the realization that you must *reward* people for reporting facts. This does not mean to pay them for informing on one another. It means to *praise men for producing factual reports* and to *criticize them for passing on rumors and vague opinions.*

Basic, also, to any worthwhile personnel information are realistic determination of the *results* an employee obtains in his work. We want to know not just what the boss or peers think of the results, but what the results are. For example: What sales volume did salesman X get last month? How much of it is new accounts? How much of his time can he account for? And so on.

Who needs to know?

At least two people need to know all about a man's results and about his past performance and present potential for the future. These are the man and his boss. The man should know what his results are, or he cannot correct them. The boss should know them, because he is responsible for them.

Executives higher up the line need not know so much about each individual employee. But they should question the boss in enough detail to be assured that he is making the information system work.

When do you collect the facts?

The system should work almost continuously. That is, a man's boss should not wait until the end of the year to sum up how well the man has been doing, but he should make notes throughout the year. If he does this, he will be astonished by the available information that he has not been using.

Having collected the facts, you still have the problem of interpreting—and, in particular, of not misinterpreting—this information. Let's look at the five common enemies of accurate analysis of personnel data.

Five Enemies of Fact Analysis

Enemy 1: Yourself.

It is easier to be subjective than objective. We would rather decide on a "hunch," quickly, and not bother with checking to see whether our facts are really facts.

Enemy 2: The Management "Politician."

Some managers have gotten where they are because of political skill. A fact-oriented system pays off for results —not vague charm.

Enemy 3: The Tired-Blood Employee.

It's easier to do things in the same old way. The tired employee would rather not be bothered with the effort required to collect facts and analyze them. Opinions and prejudices require no new thinking.

Enemy 4: The Hater, or the Neurotic.

Some managers have built up a backlog of hatred for others. They will object to facts, because the facts will run counter to some of their pet hates.

Enemy 5: The Person Studied.

The man being studied will often complain because he may be afraid the information will be misused. He may think he has more to lose than to gain. He may think the system is a way for management to spy on him.

Personnel Facts Check Sheet

Here is an outline to help you get facts about people, analyze them, and come up with the right answers.

1. What's the decision to be made?

[   ] hire   [   ] transfer
[   ] fire   [   ] discipline
[   ] promote   [   ] give a pay raise
[   ] give more authority   [   ] or other

2. To make this decision, what do you need to know about the man?

YES   NO
[   ] [   ] his performance on the job?
_____ tops   _____ below average
_____ above average   _____ unacceptable
[   ] [   ] his relations with people?
_____ close   _____ friendly
_____ distant   _____ unfriendly
[   ] [   ] his background?
_____ experience   _____ family background
_____ education   _____ outside activities
[   ] [   ] his hopes and plans for the future?

3. To get at the *specifics* of any or all of the above what information sources can you use?

YES   NO
[   ] [   ] Talk to the man himself
[   ] [   ] Review his file
[   ] [   ] Review your correspondence
[   ] [   ] Review the records about his job
             performance
[   ] [   ] Talk to his customers or associates

4. What *are* the specific facts?

5. Check your objectivity:

    YES   NO
    [ ]   [ ] Are the "facts" in 4 really specific: Do they tell Who, What, When, Where, How?
    [ ]   [ ] Did you use all the sources in 3 which are possible and feasible?

6. Do you know the man well enough to make the decision?

    YES   NO
    [ ]   [ ] If you checked on all the four areas listed in 2, you probably have a 3-D impression of him.

7. Make the decision.

To Sum Up

To avoid friction and to test the "fact-ness" of reports about people, you ask questions or make observations to pin down the Who, Where, What, and When—just as a lawyer or journalist might do. To stimulate others to be more accurate and more factual, you commend them when they produce facts, you fail to commend them or you even criticize them when they pass on rumors, opinion, and gossip.

WHAT'S THE DECISION YOU HAVE TO MAKE?	Whether, when, or how to _____

WHAT DO YOU NEED TO KNOW, TO MAKE THIS DECISION?

	What does he himself say about this?	What does his personnel file say?	What is in your correspondence file?	What do the records show about his sales etc?	What do his associates and/or customers say?
His performance on the job?					
His relations with people?					
His background and experience?					
His hopes, plans, attitude toward the future?					

TEST EVERY FACT HERE: Does it tell Who, What, Where, When, How, How Much?

ARE YOU, THEN, READY TO MAKE THE DECISION?	Yes: I am (or am not) going to _____

A System for Checking Facts

Five enemies of accurate personnel fact-analysis are: yourself (your own prejudices); the "politician" (substitutes charm for accuracy); the tired employee (avoids the effort); the hater, or neurotic, (fights for pet hates); and the individual under observation (fears the analysis).

While you cannot always overcome all these obstacles, you can go a long ways toward improving the "fact-analysis climate" of your organization by systematizing your collection and analysis of the data about a person. The format shown in this chapter is applicable to most situations; however, you should modify it and add to it in order to make it fit your company and your specific situation.

how to

Use Clues and Motives to
Make Better Decisions

THE GOOD FARMERS OF PENNSYLVANIA PLOUGHED their lands for years without knowing that a fortune in oil was underfoot. Similarly, in business a thousand useful facts lie around waiting for someone to translate them into decisions that will be profitable. This is the responsibility and reward of the successful executive.

Let's consider a case in which you can, by using some imagination and concentration, make sense of what you see. Then we will outline a broader approach which you can apply to many situations.

The Case of the Too-High
Accident Rate

Stan Slack, Safety Manager for the Dobson Company, was faced with rising accident rates. The insurance company warned him repeatedly that their premium would be raised. However, Stan seemed unable to persuade the operating managers to put enough emphasis on safety.

Finally, Stan and Mr. McArdle of the insurance company met with Mr. Powell, the President of the Dobson

149

Company, and together made it plain that something had to be done about the accident rate.

The President asked Stan, "What is causing all this rise in accidents?" Stan answered, "Sir, I don't want to name names, but it seems obvious to me that the operating managers are not pushing safety—not giving it high priority. I can't make them do it because I don't have enough authority." The President said, "We'll fix that!"

Mr. Powell did two things: 1. He called a meeting of the operating managers, at which meeting Stan and Mr. McArdle "talked turkey" to the managers; and 2. He promoted Stan to *General* Manager of Safety Services. At the same meeting, Stan also stated that the operating managers were not doing their jobs properly unless and until they gave full attention to safety matters.

Predictions

With the few facts that you know, which of the following do you think will happen? More than one thing can result:

[   ]   a. There will be a gradual drop in the accident rates.

[   ]   b. There will be a continued rise in the accident rates.

[   ]   c. There will be resentment against the insurance company, which later will mean the insurance company will lose its contract with the Dobson Company.

[ ] d. Some managers will complain that Stan got his promotion for "non-performance" *i.e.*, because there were too many accidents.

[ ] e. The operating managers look at the newly promoted Stan with new respect.

Make your decision before you read what actually happened. (Consider what you have been told, and review the alternatives above. Either a or b occurred, but c, d, or e, or some combination of them may also have occurred.)

Actual results

The following happened:

1. Alternative a occurred, but only as a gradual reduction in the accident rates. Was it caused by Stan's new aggressiveness, or from other reasons? It is difficult to be sure, but probably Stan stimulated and hastened already existing factors.
2. Alternative b obviously did not occur.
3. Alternative c occurred. There was resentment against the insurance company, and it lost the account a year later.
4. Alternative d occurred. Other managers complained that Stan was "the first man they had met in the company who had been promoted because he had not performed well."
5. Alternative e occurred in part. There was some evidence that operating managers listened more carefully

to Stan after the meeting, but it could not be said that they looked on him with much greater respect.

Four Clues to the Predictions

What were the four clues to pick up in this case?

1. *The drop in accident rates.* Mr. McArdle of the insurance company, a specialist in such matters, thought the accident rate *could* be brought down. And Stan Slack as an experienced safety manager was staking his career on bringing them down. Both had agreed upon the plan of action. This evidence predicts that the rates *could* and *would* come down.

2. *The resentment toward the insurance company.* The insurance agent was in a difficult position. His interest in safety was sincere, but his inspectors were outsiders to the company employees. Wouldn't the President resent the "public" report of safety failures in his company and the threatened rise in premiums? Wouldn't the operating managers react adversely to the "public" criticism they got from Stan and Mr. McArdle at the meeting? Perhaps such resentment will not always be translated into cancelled contracts, but you can bet that the people involved would not enthusiastically support a renewal of the contracts.

3. *Some operations managers complained that Stan got his promotion for "non-performance."* Mr. Powell, the President, gave no other reasons for Stan's promotion except that the accident rates were too high. The managers resented the criticisms they got from Stan and wanted to strike back at him, logically or not. The

President should have used better timing; he should have waited until the rates came down before promoting Stan.

4. *Stan did not gain prestige immediately*. It takes years, either before or after a promotion, to build the accompanying prestige. In this case everyone realized that Stan's fortunes stood or fell with the safety rate he might or might not obtain.

What to Do About Cases
of This Kind

Was this situation properly handled? Yes—in terms of the accident rates; they came down. No—in terms of the insurance company; they did a good job, but lost the account. No—in terms of Stan's own career; he did a good job but did not, frankly, enhance his own position very much. No—in terms of company policy; a man like Stan who does a good job should afterward be recognized and rewarded. Stan got his recognition and reward *before* the accident rates came down.

Regardless of the best way to deal with a case of this kind, the main point to be gained is to learn to spot the clues to success or failure before they happen. Then you can change your approach before it is too late. There are plenty of clues to spot and use in any such case.

Applying the Clues to
Other Cases

The real point of the foregoing case is that we learn to make sense by following up what happens and then working back to the original facts. We can then see how to use the clues properly.

What kinds of clues to look for

Usually, the most important clues are those related to people's feelings. Therefore, in regard to each man in a case, ask at least the following questions:

1. What is he trying to do?
2. How does this situation affect his self-esteem?
3. How will he probably react?

For example, in the Stan Slack case the important characters were: Stan, the safety manager; the operating managers; Mr. McArdle, the insurance representative; the President, Mr. Powell.

What were the possible feelings of each person? Here you will have to make some rough guesses based on your experience with most safety managers, most insurance representatives, most presidents, and most operating managers. When you know the individuals in real life, your estimates will be quite accurate. Here, you have to make assumptions about how they would react.

We can reasonably agree that Stan felt threatened because his job was not going well. The same would be true to some degree in regard to the insurance man, the president, the operating managers.

You might think the managers would be grateful to Stan when it turned out that, sure enough, the rates could be lowered by forthright action on their part. Perhaps this is the way some managers react. But some also react with resentment. They got the accident rates down but were not happy with Stan—or with the insurance agency that, in their eyes, "started all the fuss."

In summary, look for two kinds of clues: (1) How each individual is likely to feel, and (2) How he is likely to regard his role in the situation and the actions expected of him.

Establish the Man's Modus Operandi

Crime experts say that each criminal has a modus operandi, a characteristic way of operating which can be discerned from the type of crimes he commits. For example, Fingers Brown works between midnight and two A.M., always wears dark glasses, is courteous to his victims, and steals only money and jewelry. On the other hand, Bugs Johnson always works with an accomplice and, when opposed, turns to rough stuff.

Every incident at work, every action taken by a manager, every opinion expressed, reveals his modus operandi. It all adds up to a pattern from which you can learn to estimate what he will do, and how best to help him.

In the equation $X + Y = Z$, let X stand for a man's feelings about his work, and Y stand for the role he thinks is expected of him; then Z will be the total result. As you may recall from your high-school algebra, the $X + Y$ equation has no solution when it appears one time. However, when it is repeated enough times, you can learn not only what the Z actually adds up to, but can recognize the proper interpretation of the X and the Y, feelings and actions.

How to Understand and Use Motives

The Chart of Basic Motives on page 157 is based on the findings of a team of outstanding behavioral scientists. The chart is based on a simple four-way division of motives into Affection vs. Hate and Dominance vs. Submissiveness. These are four basic ways we treat others. A manager's modus operandi is based largely on these four motives or combinations of them.

Affection

The motive of the affectionate person is to be with people and to show that he feels positively toward them. A salesman usually has to have a great deal of this motivation. In other kinds of jobs, caring about people may or may not be an ingredient to business success. Our point here is that you should recognize the motive when you encounter it, because it can have great significance when you are estimating what a man will do, and what the reactions of others will be.

Submissiveness

The motive of the submissive person is to be with people and to *do* something for them, especially to do what they wish. The willingness to be a subordinate doesn't necessarily mean *feeling* subordinate. One can be a subordinate without being *servile*. The difference between subordinates who serve willingly and those who are servile can be a key point in understanding their behavior. It is a matter of the degree of

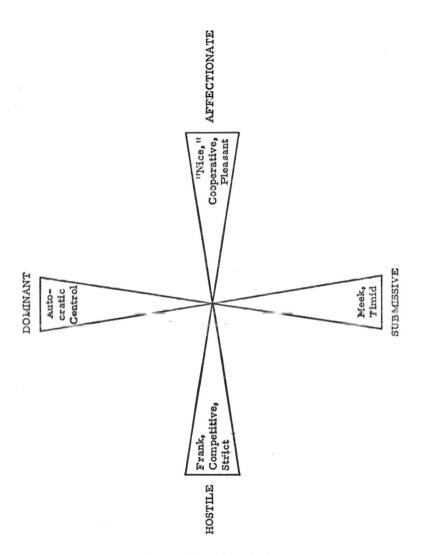

Chart of Basic Motives

the motive. The servile subordinate possesses this motive to such an intense degree that it dominates his performance.

Dominance

The motive of the dominant person is to get people to do what he wishes. In many respects, this motive is the opposite of submissiveness. It is not purely the opposite, however, because in an organization it is no use having managers who can give orders but can't take them. There are managers who show a great deal of dominance, but also show enough submissiveness to wish to carry out corporate policies.

A common impression of the manager is that he tends to dominate people to the point where he does all their thinking for them. Not so, as far as countless good managers are concerned; nevertheless, you should be alert to recognize the manager whose overwhelming desire to control people causes him to allow them no initiative.

Hate

The motive of the hostile (or hating) person is to act against other people— to show them up in some way (and hence to make himself look good), or at least to prevent them from taking advantage of him. A man who is afraid of his competitors to an exaggerated degree is a good example.

It is not unusual to be fearful of what others will do. All of us have had experiences indicating that some people can't be trusted. The hostile (or hate) motive is not uncommonly the result.

The question, again, is how much of this motive a man shows. If it is too intense, it blots out constructive thinking. Milder amounts, however, create useful rivalries and a competitive attitude. Most sales managers have at least a mild degree of competitive tendencies.

Effects on others

The motives others see in us lead them to behave in certain ways. For example, one person's motives exert a certain "pull" on other people's motives. Dominance tends to pull submissiveness from one's subordinates. Competitiveness tends to pull competitiveness. Affection tends to pull affection.

The point is not that there is a fixed pattern of reactions to use (for example, sometimes competitiveness pulls submissiveness), but that other people help keep us "in character." The manager's modus operandi is caused not only by his own actions but by the way other managers and employees *react* to the "pull" of those actions.

Stan's Motives: From Two Viewpoints

Stan Slack's motives as he saw them: Stan saw himself as exercising firm leadership. He believed that to get results he had to dominate the operating managers. Hence, he hit them hard at the meeting, with the President to back him up!

Stan's motives as the managers saw them: The managers felt, however, that Stan was trying to make them look bad in front of the President. To Stan, the motivation was domination; but to them, he was competing with them for the favor of the President, trying to make them look responsible for the company's high accident rates.

Reconciliation of motives: Perhaps the most tragic fact of human motivation is the inability of a person to see his motivations as others do. Our actions do not *feel* the same way to others as they *feel* to ourselves.

How can we reconcile our motives and the motives others see in us, and vice versa? This is a basic problem in the development of managers. The first thing to do is to accept that this difference does exist, and that it can cause you serious problems. The second thing is to look for what others see in us.

Recapitulation

Let's recapitulate the ideas covered so far:

CLUES: Your everyday work is filled with clues which can tell you about others and yourself. Look for the modus operandi, a man's typical motives. Look also for the reactions his motives "pull" from others.

FEELINGS: Look for the clues that tell you how a person feels about his work and his relations with others.

ROLES: Look for the clues that tip you off as to what a person thinks is *expected* of him—what role in the business he believes he is supposed to play. His intensity of feelings and the roles he adopts in the business lead him to show certain motivations which make up his modus operandi.

MOTIVES: The clues eventually add up to an overall picture which we call *motives*. A manager's motives can be grouped under four major headings or combinations: affection, hostility, dominance, and submission.

OUTSIDE VS. INSIDE: In any situation, you can pick up clues to four different things: your own motives as you see them; your own motives as others see them; their motives as they see them; and theirs as you see them.

Six Steps to Becoming a Top Motivator of People

Why is it hard to learn to motivate people? It isn't hard at all if you take the right approach. It is next to impossible if you take the wrong approach. Let's start with some Don't's and then move on to some Do's.

1. Don't think of motivating people as a matter of learning how to push the right buttons.

   People are not puppets. They are not machines with levers. They are not dogs, cats, or horses to be trained to respond to your every whim.

2. Don't expect that people will see you as you see yourself.

   People react to their own motives and feelings and roles, as well as to what you are doing. They hear what you say according to their own mood of the moment—not according to yours.

3. For every action you see another man take in business, ask *why;* look for the motive.

Why? is one of the most valuable questions in all business. It will lead to insights. It will uncover new facts. It is curiosity put to practical use.

4. Build up a picture of each man's motives, feelings, and roles.

Especially in selling, it is almost impossible to operate without some idea of why a customer does what he does, and how he characteristically reacts to what you say. It is true in all other phases of business.

5. Notice how people react to your own motives. What do they do when you speak or act in your own typical modus operandi?

6. Recognize that in some situations you have been self-defeating, and then take an entirely fresh approach.

Your competitiveness may have been creating rivalries where you don't want them. Your domination may have been inspiring servile obedience where you want initiative. Your cooperativeness may have been opening the door to others who believe from this that you are soft and easy to control. Your own loyal relationships to your superior may have been seen by him as a lack of authority and drive. This last point has led many a good second man to be passed over for promotion, as the company brings in an outsider . who looks more aggressive.

Summary

All business decisions are the outcomes of someone's analysis of the data of the situation and translation of its import into action terms. All business decisions also involve predictions about how people will behave. To make such decisions, an executive must learn to spot the clues to the future—the roles that men typically play and the emotional forces that motivate them.

In regard to clues and roles, one can play the detective and by reviewing a person's past action discover his modus operandi; that is, his customary way of behaving in a situation. Above all, one must learn to seee human behavior from two viewpoints: (1) as seen by the individual himself, and (2) as seen and felt by others.

handling

Special Decision Situations

Dealing with the
Under-25 Group

During the coming years, the increase in the number of men and women workers under 25 will be tremendous. They will constitute a group requiring many decisions: hiring, firing, disciplining, motivating, extending or refusing to them "personnel credit" as well as financial credit. Pertinent to remember about them are:

- They have had little or no business or job experience.
- They are mobile. They "job hop"—they move from place to place, making it difficult to show a record of consistent income or job performance.
- They are often on the defensive, unsure of themselves, and not easy to communicate with.

However, they enter the labor market the best educated in history. In the mid 1960's more than half of the high school graduates go to college; this per cent is increasing and will increase for the foreseeable future.

165

Three Checks on the Young
Candidate

Three quick tips for appraising the potential job performance of the under-25 employee are:

1. Check his college or high school transcript. If you want brains, look for A grades with a sprinkling of B's. If you want a steady performer, look for the straight B man. Remember that few men can be good in everything; hence, an A in creative writing or political science offsets a C or even D in physics or accounting, and vice versa. Other things being equal, a man with several A's and a few D's is usually a better choice than one with straight C's, because it shows he has high potential in certain areas, while the other fellow is just mediocre all-around.

   Schools vary in their methods of grading, so find out how the man stood in his class and also ask people familiar with the school about its standards. Does it give B's where other schools give C's, or vice versa?

2. Find out what he did, if anything, that indicated leadership and human-relations ability:
   Did he hold campus office?
   Did he participate in any social groups?
   Was he an athlete?

3. If he had military training:
   Was he assigned to key jobs, or did he just put in his time until he "got his military service out of the way"?

Was he assigned to service training schools? (This indicates that his military supervisors and classifiers believed he had the aptitude and willingness to learn.)

Did he achieve commissioned or noncommissioned rank?

Was he discharged under honorable conditions?

Use the Credit Manager's Approach

When you are thinking about giving a young person key opportunities or key duties, ask yourself, "What would I want to know about him before lending him money?"

Look at past repayments on investments of financial or personnel credit in the man. The principle here is one which we have stressed throughout this book: People tend to do in the future what they have done in the past. Apply it on two levels: money-wise, you trust people who pay their bills; personnel-wise, you look at the past performance as the basis for estimating future performance. How did the man produce? How did he keep his word?

Look at reasons for wanting the money, job, or assignment. The loan-maker has the right to know the reasons for the loan, because the motive of the person is a leading clue to repayment. The principle here is also one which is stressed throughout this book: People are constantly motivated by one need or another, and knowing a man's motives means knowing the man's future performance. Therefore, a man with a mature and considered reason for seeking a loan, job, or assignment is more likely to honor his obligations. That is, find out *why* he wants a career in your organization or a promotion.

Look at his long-range intentions. Most people when they are asking for loans *intend* to repay them. But most people hate to look ahead. Ask any insurance salesman how hard it is to get a 25-year-old to buy life insurance! The principle here is: People plan out their future to some extent, and knowing the plans provides important clues to what they will do. How can you apply this principle to making decisions about young people? Ask the young man where he wants to go in his career, and what he is going to have to do to get there. If he gives a vague answer, you probably can't make an accurate forecast more than a year or so in advance. If he can outline to you a sensible plan for becoming a top corporate officer in 20 years, you've got a good prospect for an investment of your time and money!

MOTIVATIONS: In general, extreme young rebels are noisy but not numerous. Most young Americans today are not fighting battles with their parents (four out of five students think their parents have handled them "about right"). Students can get excited over current issues; but on the whole, the modern student seems to be serious, only occasionally "busting loose."

The average college student is probably higher in competitiveness and frankness in interpersonal relations and in motivations than in 1940 or earlier generations. He is perhaps more dependent, in the sense of being able to work under the authority of others; but this doesn't mean he is a docile employee. He had been taught to fight hard to achieve something, and this achievement desire may be more important in his eyes than just having a job.

ABILITIES: The under-25 employee is likely to be fast-thinking, intelligent, and potentially creative. He is better than his father was in terms of knowing how to express himself.

Many creative achievements appear among the people between 19 and 25. For instance, in the physical sciences many of the "break-throughs" have come from the very young scientists; many artists and composers have had successes in, or even before, their twenties. Don't underestimate the abilities of the under-25 generation. Take advantage of their abilities by giving chances to show what they can do.

On the other hand, while the under-25 group is the group that composes the most poetry and smashes atoms, it is also the group with high accident rates, high crime rates, high potentials for trouble.

Decision Check List for Young Employees

DECISION:	CHECK TO MAKE:
1. Shall I hire this young person?	What does his school, military, athletic, and leadership record say about his abilities and motives? Have you cross-checked the school record against your own interview impressions and against the results of your own personnel tests?

2. Shall I give him a chance as a management trainee?

Has he used his opportunities in the past? If not, why do you think he will, now?

Do you know why he is working in your organization? Money is a necessary reason, but it is not enough of a motive alone for business success.

Does he have a career plan? If he is a "drifter" in handling his own life, chances are he will drift as a manager.

3. How much responsibility can he be given?

You are more likely to underestimate the abilities of this group than to overestimate them; therefore, you may be risking waste from under-responsibility and under-use.

Have you tested out the individual younger person's willingness to carry a heavier load?

4. How important is money as a motive? When should raises be given?

Are you paying the going rate for college graduates?

Are you aware that the current under-25 generation is strongly motivated by grades and other signs of achievement? If you can't find some other "signs of progress," you may have to pay cash premiums for this age group of employees.

	Are you honestly paying for achievement, or do you ignore the job results of the man because of his youth?
5. What about discipline?	Is the skylarking, absenteeism, or general "goofing off" due to lack of sound supervision? Have you assigned enough challenge and enough responsibility to the young ones?
6. How about turnover?	The turnover of employees this age is partly due to their being single, low on the management totem-pole and with little to lose by moving around. But part of the turnover will be due to the supervision and the climate given them. Try hiring the married ones, and try transferring the restless young man within the company, rather than waiting for him to "transfer himself" to another company.

Handling the Creative Employee

The number of jobs that demand more mind than muscle increases every year. It is doubtful that there are or will be enough creative people to fill the present or future creative jobs. And basic to the problem is the attitude of *man-*

agement toward creativity. If management doesn't encourage creative thinking, doesn't permit it on the job, doesn't use the ideas after they have been born, talk about creativity is useless.

If you are near the top of a company, or head up a department, you have life-and-death power over the new ideas that bubble up from your subordinates. Men who produce new ideas, whether in sales, or engineering, or production, have a *creative limit*. This *limit* is the number of no answers a man will take before he stops suggesting ideas. To make the matter worse, some of the hare-brained ideas that may cross your desk (if you permit any at all) *are* actually destructive.

New ideas develop in response to one or more of the following questions:

1. What new uses can I find for this thing?
2. How can I change this for the better?
3. What can I substitute for this thing?
4. What can I add to, subtract from, multiply, or divide?
5. How can I rearrange, reverse, or pep up this thing?

The man who asks those questions is asking them about a policy, product, procedure, or principle which you may have introduced or you may have lived with for a long time. Therefore, he dares to interfere with what you are proud of or have learned to live with. To you, he is destructive!

Creative work tears down, alters, or criticizes what has been done before. This annoys the boss or older manager who happens to believe there is some merit in what has been done before. It annoys a young manager who admires or profits from changing the old way of doing things.

Creative environments may be different

A greeting-card manufacturer has a department whose sole responsibility is producing new designs. Some of the designers wear goatees and berets to work. They keep odd working hours, take coffee breaks at almost any time, and the whole atmosphere appears most unbusinesslike; but the department produces.

A person trying to do a creative job may be unconventional in other things in order to think differently. The manager who won't let his designers wear goatees may interfere with their thinking and, thereby, interfere with their production—the production of ideas. Limits have to be set for every part of business life; but for creative workers, the limits must be broader than the manager may find suitable for himself and for routine workers.

Psychological profiles of creative people

MOTIVATIONS. What typical motivational patterns do creative workers show? Probably all kinds of people are capable of creative ideas. But the typically creative person tends to be the person who insists on thinking for himself, who places great value on his own ideas, on "not going along with the crowd." He is the person about whom others say: "He resents being bossed." "He's moody at times." "He's a complainer, who doesn't like the way things are done." "He's touchy, and easily hurt."

He is also often competitive, in the sense of placing

great emphasis on his ideas, his career, and his ability to excel along lines chosen by himself. His musical, artistic, or literary tastes are also different. He prefers complexity, abstract painting, jazz, or folk music; he is an intellectual, though not in the sense of being a Phi Beta Kappa or having a high I. Q.

ABILITIES. The creative person will show flashes of brilliance in the subjects in which he has a special interest. His college record will be spotty. When you talk with him, he will at times get onto a subject obscure to you but in which he is astonishingly well-read. He has special abilities (some day you may have special need of them) and a capacity for imagination that can solve problems your steady, dependable people cannot solve.

Decision Check List for Creative Employees

DECISIONS:

CHECK TO MAKE:

1. How can I hire more creative people? Or spot the ones already working for me?

Does this man have enough experience on which to base useful ideas, but is he still skeptical enough to keep that experience from blocking the new ideas?

Is he like everybody else you have on the payroll, or is he different in tastes?

Does he have the courage to think up and present ideas that will "rock the boat"?

2. How much control should I keep over my creative people?

Are you *stifling* ideas? Is your company's production rate of new ideas equal to or better than that of other businesses?

What is your ratio of Noes to Yeses when people make suggestions? (Have you tried teaching your people to accept a certain number of Noes as inevitable in business life?)

3. When to fire a creative employee?

Are you firing people for just rocking the boat on nonessentials?

Creative people are fired faster than other kinds of employees—are *you* firing the creative ones faster than the "loyal dopes"? Why?

4. Do your promotion policies favor creative managers?

Watch out for: 1. Promoting people only because they resemble you; 2. Promoting men because they do not make trouble; and 3. Promoting too many men of the same kind.

While many noncreative people are needed and should be promoted, there should be a substantial percentage who can think up new approaches to new and old problems.

5. How can I be sure that creativity is properly emphasized?	Find the key areas in which your business needs to make faster improvements.
	Don't regard only the *key* jobs of the company as the "think jobs." Review all jobs for creative potential.
	Look over the job descriptions written by the Personnel Department and start taking out the nit-picking duties and replace them with things that count more.
	Your company was founded by a creative man. Have you let that kind of thinking go out of style?

Hiring and Working With the Older Employee

Older employees are also increasing in number—especially the women over 35 years of age. This group contrasts with the young and the creative employees in that many older employees *seem* to oppose anything which is new.

However, this is not due to the physical aging but the change in their motives and abilities. Remember this and you can do much to help the older group to remain fully productive and, in some cases, creative.

Older employees may not think as fast as younger ones, but this is mainly because they check new ideas against their "bank account of ideas" from the past. In many situations, such caution is valuable.

The creative output of the older scientist tends to be slower than that of younger scientists. But this is not a black-and-white difference. Benjamin Franklin, for example, started serious experimentation with electricity after the age of 40.

Four causes of conservatism in older workers

The older employee opposes change because:

1. He has worked in an atmosphere of seniority, status, and authority and feels he has more to lose from a change than he has to gain (and this may be true).

2. He sees pitfalls and unfavorable side-effects in a new idea which the younger employee does not see (and they may truly be there).

3. If he is near retirement age, perhaps he can see no reason for struggle (while a younger employee still feels he has "the world to win").

4. He is illness-prone, and this makes him cautious about extending himself.

Authority-bias in older workers

In a position of authority, the older employee tends toward the autocratic, a type of motivation that inspires either meekness in his subordinates or sub-surface rebellion and opposition. (Our motivations always evoke motivations from others, but not always the ones we want them to have!)

If he is very authoritarian, the older manager thinks things like the following: "People don't have the initiative they need to have." (He doesn't realize that their meekness is at least partly in reaction to his own autocratic manner.) Or, "People oppose authority too much and don't acknowledge the prerogatives of management." (He doesn't realize that rebelliousness is also natural reaction to his autocratic manner.)

The authoritarian, older manager under pressure tends to tighten controls, to criticize, to fire people. This approach makes the meek ones meeker, the rebellious ones more rebellious.

Older women

Under the right conditions, a woman with the right background and abilities can become a successful manager. However, the requirements for background, abilities, and motivational requirements are not met in many instances. Most top jobs demand higher levels of education, and women are "school dropouts" at a higher rate than men are. A woman takes time out to raise a family; and when she gets back to a business career, she has a 10-to 20-year disadvantage compared to the men who have been able to stick at it.

One old-wives' tale (believed by men about women) is that women work primarily for pin-money. They don't need the jobs as men do, so the argument runs, and a weaker male candidate is promoted over the head of a stronger managerial candidate who happens to be female. There are women who work for pin-money, but there are also millions of women who are the heads of families: they are single, divorced, or widowed. They need the money and their job motivations are just like those of men.

Another old-wives' tale (maybe we had better call it an old-duffers' tale) is that women are too temperamental. This observation is based on the fact that in our culture it is OK for women to cry. Men "blow their stacks," but the old-duffers don't brand that as "temperamental." Often men don't express their feelings as freely as women, and this may be why the ulcer rate and heart attack rate are several times higher among men than among women.

Psychological Profile of Older Men

What we have said about older men boils down to the following assets and limitations.

On the positive side

ABILITIES	More deliberate in evaluating new ideas, comparing them with other ideas in their "bank of experience." Ability to accept responsibility.
MOTIVES	Greater desire to remain with the same company. Desire to keep the operation under control and to hold on to the benefits already gained by the past company policies, products, etc.

On the negative side

ABILITIES   Slow to accept new ideas and, in general, slowed-down reaction-time mentally and physically.

Slowed down in energy and increasingly prone to health problems.

MOTIVES   Motivated to protect what he has rather than to encourage new ideas for the good of the company.

Tends to overcontrol people.

Psychological Profile of Older Women

Older women share the abilities and motives listed for older men. In addition, they have assets and limitations of their own.

On the positive side

ABILITIES   A greater understanding of consumer motivations. (Women spend 90 per cent of the nation's household money and know how such decisions are made.)

MOTIVES   Greater flexibility in managerial styles. (Men tend towards autocratic methods; women are more willing to use other methods for getting people to do things.)

On the negative side

ABILITIES   Many women are career dropouts and are behind men of the same age in education and experience.

MOTIVES   It is harder for a woman to avoid dividing her interest between home and work.

Decision Check Chart for Older Employees

DECISION:	CHECK POINTS:
1. Should I hire older people?	In jobs demanding the abilities and motivations of older persons— *yes*, (Particularly where lower accident rates, lower turnover, and lower absenteeism are important.)
2. What can be done to prevent over - 45 employees from resisting change?	Resistance to change is not directly caused by age; check the specific reasons such an employee fears change: loss of status or seniority, etc. Give him advance warning about the proposed move before it is made. Involve him in organizing the change, rather than in merely taking a stand on whether it is good or bad.
3. Do we need a special policy on jobs for women? Promotion? Pay?	Do women want favored status? We do not recommend this as desirable. Try analyzing women's abilities

and motivations in the same terms that you have your male employees: there are more similarities than differences.

4. Is mandatory retirement a good idea for our company?	Set a firm date, otherwise, people can't or won't plan for retirement. Mandatory retirement, however, is unfair unless there is a provision for a pension plan.
5. Is it wise to cut off promotions at certain age levels?	A lot of the "conservatism" of older employees is due to their opinion that they can't advance any further. Be slow to tell a man he cannot advance further.

Summary

Young employees tend toward competitiveness, frankness, and (sometimes) dependency; older employees tend toward greater emphasis on autocratic attitudes. The young ones think more quickly; the older ones think more comprehensively.

The younger group may show more creativity, but creativity can be found (or stimulated) at all ages. Creativity belongs at all levels of management, and it results more from the person's outlook and motivation than from his education, experience, or position.

Success in making the best use of the old or young, the creative or the conservative, lies in matching the man to the job. However, we all tend to confuse the facts of the situations with the stereotypes we carry in our minds. Hence, this chapter has presented psychological profiles and decision check charts to help you sort out the salient features of the young, the old, and the creative person, vis-à-vis the jobs most suitable for him or her.

how to

Establish a Strong
Decision-Making Pattern

Reduce Confusion by Following
a Pattern Approach

Most of the confusion in a business comes from human confusion. To reduce this confusion you need to develop an approach, a pattern that will bring order. A five-ring circus appears extremely complex, even riotous to the audience; but an experienced ringmaster can see the underlying pattern, and not be confused. Chapter 6 presented the basic pattern, the DPC cycle: observe, analyze, and predict. Subsequent chapters discussed what to observe, how to analyze, and how to predict.

This chapter will provide you with a step-by-step approach to ensure that you get the most out of this basic decision-making pattern. It's not enough to know what to do, you must also motivate yourself and others to stick with the "pattern approach" (like an airplane pilot practicing landings) until you and they can act smoothly and expeditiously.

185

Remember:

> *In learning any new skill, you must accept some initial stumbling and fumbling. Don't let yourself be discouraged.*

Four Steps and Their Sub-Steps

Step One: Start keeping records

Too busy to write things down? Some businessmen, a few decades ago, said the same thing about accounting records. They were "too busy" running the business to take time out to write down their expenditures and income.

● *If your company has no system of personnel records, start one.* Keep it simple, but start it. What ought to be in the personnel records? Clues to each man's motives and abilities, such as:

1. Past experience in other jobs and/or with other companies.

2. His results on his present job, preferably measured by the practical business yardsticks of profit and loss, sales volume, control of waste, and maintenance of customer relations.

3. His relations with people on his present job: people below him in authority, on his own level, above him in authority, and both inside and outside the company.

4. His ambitions, hopes, and plans for the future. *Remember*: one dimension" of a man is his future!

• *If your company has no system of keeping records on customer contacts, start one.* If you have many small customers, start a record of "typical customers." What ought to be in your customer record? Clues to the customers' wants, what they will and will not buy.

1. The "history" of your customers: their past performances; their resources; rate of growth and potential for the future.
2. What they are thinking today about your product.
3. Their relationships with your representatives.

(Note the 3-D picture of the customer as a person. What has he done, how does he react now, and where does he seem to be heading?)

• *If you are in a staff department, set up a "customer record" on the line managers you service. What ought to be in this record?*

1. The things these "customers" want from your department—the nature and volume of their past requests, complaints, or compliments.
2. Pressures and problems in those departments.
3. Their relationships with yourself or your representatives.
4. Information concerning their future plans and objectives.

(Does it hurt your pride to look at your associates as "customers?" It shouldn't. Ask yourself: Would the other departments in my company purchase my department's services at my overhead rate if they had to purchase these services from outside the business? You may get a shock.)

Step Two: Force feedback into your records

Now, we come to the man-sized part of the job. Step Two takes nerve, because it requires you to face results you might prefer to forget.

- *Start putting your decisions about people into the records.*

1. Do this every day. Most contacts with people inside or outside your business will result in a decision by you to do or not to do something. So, write it down: hire, fire, promote, sell, discipline, reward, and so forth.
2. Be frank and dare to make blunt predictions. Otherwise you will have no opportunity to check your success or failure or to learn to face up to firm decisions.
3. Indicate why you made the decision.
4. Put a "call-up-date" for the results to show. The call-up might say "Tomorrow," or it might say "January, next year."

Set up a system for automatically following up each decision on a certain date. The figure on page 189 shows a form for an operational tickler file that also provides you with a way to learn from your experience. It gives you information about how well your decisions are getting results.

Make this system automatic by putting a square of carbon paper to the right of the vertical dotted line. Clip the carbon copy along each dotted line, making three coupons. The original copy stays in your records for January 15 (shows what the decision was). The coupons (carbon copies of the original dates) should be placed in your desk calendar on each follow-up date. When March 15 turns up, you will see a coupon which says that a decision made on January 15 is to be checked on March 15. On January 22, you will follow up to ask, 1. Will the Smith Company give us back our account? On March 15, you will follow up to ask, 2. IIow well is Jones managing the western depots? On June 15, you will follow up to ask, 3. Is Davis making enough progress toward the goal of 10 per cent improvement in his sales?

DECISION:	Date of Decision	Follow-up Date
● Let Jones manage the western depots...........	January 15	March 15
● Write the Smith Co. about the account we lost; offer them a discount...................	January 15'	January 22
● Put Davis on notice that he will have to improve his sales 10% by the end of the year........	January 15	June 15

For each decision, decide whether in fact you are getting the results you forecast. If you do these things, you are forcing feedback into your records. This makes good business sense. But let's consider the pitfalls that cause an executive to drop a feedback system before it has a chance to pay off.

How People Make Feedback
Systems Fail

Under pressure of time, the Kretz Company changed some of its production equipment in order to fill orders for a new tube-liner. The production staff worked hard, visiting all 18 plants, meeting with the foremen, explaining the change, and establishing goals. When they finished installing the change in one plant, they immediately moved on to the next. In this way they covered all 18 plants in nine weeks.

What happened? The waste materials from wrong equipment settings and confused personnel mounted to $200,000 a month. The tube-liner sales increase met the forecast made by the sales vice-president, but the profits were more than consumed by the waste costs. Everyone got pretty edgy about the situation.

The basic cause? The production staff had to move from installing the change in one plant to the next plant, and were on such a tight schedule that they could not return to preceding plants to help trouble-shoot the inevitable confusions and break-downs. The local plants were not strong enough to do such trouble-shooting themselves. You could say local plant personnel deficiencies were the long-range cause. But the immediate cause was the lack of feedback of results on each change obtained soon enough to make a correction before making the change in the next plant. Neither the production department nor the sales department allowed adequately for feedback.

Several reasons why managers won't obtain or use feedback properly—why they cause feedback systems to fail—can be seen in this example:

Time pressure: One of the first things sacrificed when deadlines are short is feedback.

Pride: In this case, the sales department believed there could be no question about the soundness of its planning and forced the production department to operate with its (the sales) schedules, rather than jointly working out deadlines; managers with excessive pride usually neglect feedback.

Wishful thinking: The production department had a notion that the system of installing the change in one plant before it had gotten well set in the preceding plant could lead to trouble but "hoped" it would not.

• *Changing managers' attitudes toward failure.* Top managers know they take risks when they make decisions, and they know these must be *calculated* risks. They are not necessarily surprised or shocked, therefore, when something goes wrong. To make a feedback system work, you have to:

1. Persuade the "bureaucrats" and the "autocrats" in your business to stop avoiding the bad news.

    Bureaucrats avoid checking up on results because they assume that if all employees will follow prescribed procedures, the operation will work 100 per cent.

    Autocrats avoid checking up on results because they assume that they have a far tighter control over the operation than they do in fact have. They count on a forceful manner and a clear directive to do the job for them, not on feedback.

2. Persuade the technocrats to start learning to manage.

A specialist (or technocrat) who believes that the right settings on the machinery and the right cost analyses are enough to get the job done, has got to learn to see that the right "settings" have to be made on the *people* also, and the right analyses of these people have got to be made.

Get the specialist to learn to look for feedback about what people are doing as well as what the equipment is doing.

3. Train yourself and subordinates to make positive use of the bad news. (We know a surgeon who practices for a difficult operation by deliberately making surgical errors on a cadaver.)

Experience means feedback, and if a manager cannot accept feedback of bad results as well as good results, he can learn nothing from experience.

If your staff shows evidence of taking the bad news seriously, don't climb all over them every time something goes wrong.

Hold skull sessions with your men. What will they do if the X account is lost? What will you do if your profits from the Southern division are too low?

**Step Three: Making use
of the feedback**

From your records you can discern why a decision did or did not have the results you expected. For example, you might see where you failed to obtain real evidence about a man's past abilities or motivations, or real evidence about his plans or intentions for the future.

Also, be as interested in finding out why decisions brought good results as well as finding out why they did not. Feedback should include good news and bad news, failures and successes.

● *At the time of your follow-up, check first for results: are you getting the results you expected?* A form for such a purpose might look like this:

Decision: Let Jones manage the western
    depot.
Date of follow-up: March 15.
Results on March 15: Jones has already cut
    40 per cent of unnecessary storage costs
    and has introduced a training program for
    the delivery-schedulers. He is moving very
    quickly, but on every account the results
    look good.
Date of next follow-up: June 15.

● *Look back at your original information to see what was right or wrong about the decision. Were the data in your records*:

Complete?	[ ] Yes	[ ] No
Accurate?	[ ] Yes	[ ] No
Relevant?	[ ] Yes	[ ] No

● *If the records were not adequate, take corrective action: adjust your current decisions on other cases so that they are.* The feedback system can help you get practical working results. But you are the one who will have to take the action.

Thus far, you have introduced written records about people; you have forced feedback into those records; and you have made practical use of the feedback. Let's consider one more step to get the pattern installed.

Step Four: Using the pattern in conferences

● *After every conference, ask yourself*:

1. What was going on in this conference; how did the members feel about what we were discussing? What were they trying to get me to do, and what were they trying to get each other to do?

    Result: You will learn to observe the motivations of people.

2. How did I feel about this conference? Was it tough for me?—if so, why? What was I trying to get these people to do?

    Result: You learn to be frank about your own motives and objectives.

3. How did *they* think I felt? Did they know what I was trying to do? Did they see my motives the same way I did?

    Result: You learn to recognize the kind of impact you are having.

• *Take ten minutes before every conference to ask yourself*:

1. What do I want to get out of this conference?
2. What do they probably want out of it?
3. What do they think I want?

Auren Uris tells about a business executive who attributed most of his success to what he called "the ten-minute edge." He always arrived ten minutes early for a conference, or in some other way saved ten minutes to prepare for it. He reported that other people often said of him, "Ed knows what he is doing in a meeting. Most of the other people waste a lot of their time just thrashing around."

• *Learn to describe human motivations in specific terms.* The following form could be used after a conference:

Human Motivation Checklist

In this conference I believe I was:	Person A showed these motives:	Person B showed these motives:
[ ] Autocratic, overbearing, dominating.	[ ] Autocratic, overbearing, dominating.	[ ] Autocratic, overbearing, dominating.
[ ] Sympathetic, with concern for feelings.	[ ] Sympathetic, with concern for feelings.	[ ] Sympathetic, with concern for feelings.
[ ] Cooperative, and unusually friendly.	[ ] Cooperative, and unusually friendly.	[ ] Cooperative, and unusually friendly.

I was (*cont.*)	Person A (*cont.*)	Person B (*cont.*)
[ ] Admiring and complimentary toward others' ideas.	[ ] Admiring and complimentary toward others' ideas.	[ ] Admiring and complimentary toward others' ideas.
[ ] Docile, letting others take the lead.	[ ] Docile, letting others take the lead.	[ ] Docile, letting others take the lead.
[ ] Quietly negativistic, indicating by silence that I did not agree.	[ ] Quietly negativistic, indicating by silence that I did not agree.	[ ] Quietly negativistic, indicating by silence that I did not agree.
[ ] Openly critical and blunt in my reactions.	[ ] Openly critical and blunt in his reactions.	[ ] Openly critical and blunt in his reactions.
[ ] Pushing forthrightly and competitively for the acceptance of my ideas.	[ ] Pushing forthrightly and competitively for the acceptance of his ideas.	[ ] Pushing forthrightly and competitively for the acceptance of his ideas.

Five Tips for Establishing the Decision-Making Pattern

1. Decide to reduce the natural confusion by introducing order into your decision-making.

2. Use the DPC cycle: observe, analyze, and predict. After you predict, you make further observations and check the results of the prediction.

3. Don't try to change everything at once; use a step-by-step approach.

Start out by keeping simple written records on people.

Then force feedback into the records by recording your decisions and following them up on a planned basis.

Improve your observations of "live" or conference situations (this is normally the hardest of the steps).

4. Make due allowance for discouragement; make positive use of even the bad news. In the long run bad news can be a vital help to your career if you learn from it.

5. Carry out these observing exercises in many conferences, not just in one. You don't learn to play golf by swinging a golf club only once.

decisions

For or Against People

People Are Your Most Important Resource and Problem

When Annie Besant, the lady savant, was reported to have exclaimed "I accept the universe!" Emerson commented, "By gad, she'd better!" Similarly, when a manager says, "I've got to work with people," the obvious reply is, "With whom else?"

As Chapter 1 pointed out, people are fundamental to business decisions. Costs don't cause themselves—people cause them. Equipment, supplies, tools don't make or lose profits; the people who make the decisions about buying, using, selling are the ones who deserve the praise or blame. Behind these people stand the executives who picked them to make the decisions.

The first step then, is to recognize the importance of decisions about people; the second step is to make up your mind that you *can* and *will* improve your ability to judge people, to hire them, assign them, promote them—or drop them. Chapters 1 and 2 urged you to:

199

1. Distinguish between *technical* (about things) and *personnel* (about people) analyses.

2. Look to the results you want achieved. For example, what will *this* decision about *this* person lead to in the way of more money, more profits, more improvements —or less costs, waste, or emotional problems.

3. Put a price tag on decisions: How much will a poor decision cost in turnover? How much will a man cost in salary and benefits over a period of time? How much will a man's decisions affect operations and the profit-and-loss statement? As a rule of thumb, plan to spend at least an hour of your time in appraising a man for every $2,000 in annual salary. Above $20,000, add another hour for every $1,000 increment in annual salary. Above $40,000, add an hour for each $500 in increment in salary.

4. Don't try to solve personnel failures by complaints, confrontations, and accusations, or by complex rule-making or "tightening up" and "cracking down." Check the methods used to select the people for the jobs they have failed in. Examine the past hiring decisions to discern the causes of the present troubles and to see what kinds of training programs are needed to improve future hiring practices.

How to Match the Job and the Man

Many generals have been criticized for preparing to fight the previous war. They presumed too blindly that the next war would be fought with the same weapons and in the same way as the last one. Similarly, many managers pick

Joe for the job, "because he knows it, and it's his turn." But jobs change. Joe may have been great in a supporting role in the past; or he knew the job in the way a spectator knows a play. When Joe is moved front and center, he flops. As the old adage goes: Promoting the best worker often means having a poor supervisor while losing your best producer.

Chapters 3, 4, and 5, therefore, discussed the types of analyses and the results-forecasting that ought to be performed before a man is assigned, reassigned, or promoted. The analyses are:

1. *Technical* analysis to see what the job involves, if it really needs to be done, and what it requires in knowledge, skill, and attitude.
2. *Organizational* analysis to see where the job should be done and by whom.
3. *Personnel* analysis to see if the candidate(s) *can* and *will* do the work.

Forecasting results is vital; otherwise you are simply authorizing a man to do what he wants to do, or what is convenient for him to do. You should forecast in two ways:

First, decide the goals your organization can reasonably expect to achieve—increased sales, reduced costs, higher production, lower personnel turnover, up-grading of work force, cut in grievances, replacement of professional staff, and so on.

Second, you decide the priorities among these goals— how soon you want them and how vital they are to your overall objectives. Then, you chart the "job specs" of the skills required to achieve each goal; e.g., management ability, sales ability, engineering ability, and so on.

Finally, you match each candidate against these "job specs."

NOTE: You do not simply "fill a vacancy" with the nearest available man. You pick the man to do the job of the future. Therefore, you include a back-up plan, a training and development plan to ensure that the man in the job is continuously up-dated and prepared for all his responsibilities and opportunities.

Master and Slave?

Abraham Lincoln said, "As I would not be a slave, neither would I be a master." Can you say the same about yourself? Or, do you tend toward what Eugene E. Jennings has called the "bicycle position"—bowed-down to those over you while peddling furiously on those below you?

Chapter 4 described the blocks to successful forecasting under the terms *wishing, ordering,* and *dependence on policy.* Let's sharpen our viewpoint that "people are not things but persons" by describing the alternative attitudes. Organizational relationships have developed thusly in the Western world:

HISTORICAL ERA	RELATIONSHIPS
Dawn of history to Middle Ages	Master and slave. (Slave is a *thing,* and he can't quit.)
Middle Ages to the Renaissance	Master and serf. (Serf is a man but with a thing's lack of rights, and he can't quit.)

Renaissance to Modern Times	Master and servant. (Servant has some rights, and he can quit.)
Modern Times	Employer and employee. (Employee can leave, and negotiates and bargains about his rights, wages, and working conditions. However, he is "below" the employer in status.)
Future	Professionals and technicians? (Machines do the work; the professionals and technicians accomplish mutually agreed upon goals under the general direction of "professional managers and executives"???)

Even the terms *employer* and *employee* have a thing-aspect about them. They can imply that the one buys the other as a commodity. Of course, when one is summarizing, abstracting, and classifying for budget and planning purposes, one has to speak of *employees* or *personnel*. But when you make decisions about *individuals,* remember that the term *employee* means more than "man at work." That man or woman has hopes and fears, needs and desires—and often some pretty shrewd notions about the way he or she is being "employed."

Four Executive Attitudes

Four attitudes on the part of an executive that can cause trouble are: the autocratic, the bureaucratic, the technocratic, and the autistic (wishful). Here's a brief review of them:

Autocratic

The autocrat confuses forecasting with policy—his policy. When he says, "The future will . . ." he means, "The following had better happen, or heads will roll!" The modern autocrat usually hides his dependence on threats and bullying by clothing his utterances in "economic" or "moral" phrases. For example, he might pontificate something like this:

> In our business we must remain ever-conscious of the power of the market. Though we try to remember the human factors involved, we cannot abrogate the laws of nature and we cannot abrogate management's primary function of deciding and implementing policy with regard to the products to be made, when to make them, and how to sell them. To date, our failures have been due to the unwillingness of people to do what they are told to do, to recognize the facts of life, and to work as hard as people used to work.

Of course, management decides the when, how, and where; but the key question is, Why did the speaker feel the need to make such statements?

At first sight, his statements may appear good, and they appeal to the autocratic sentiments in all of us. But examine them more closely. They are redundant and meaningless, unless someone is having doubts about how effectively the management has been performing! Moreover, such statements imply a distinction between *business* decisions and *human* decisions. But business decisions must be carried out by human beings! For instance, a forecast of sales is meaningless unless one also plans the what, why, and how of the persons who accomplish the advertising, promotion, customer relations, and distribution of the merchandise.

Moralizings about how people don't work so hard anymore may or may not be founded in fact. If not, why talk about it? But even if true, the more useful approach would be to list the steps that one must take to get people to work harder. Or, one might propose doing the work by machines, or by contracting it out, or by reassigning responsibilities. Whether the moralizings are true or not, they signal that the speaker feels frustrated because people are not doing things his way. He confuses complaining about a problem with solving it and wastes his energies and others' eardrums accordingly.

Therefore, when you find yourself saying, "People are no good . . . ," or "These employees can't be trusted . . . ," stop and start again with: "Because these persons are not producing the results we desire, we must take steps to change their—and our—approach, attitude, or method. Now, which changes in processes, job assignments, motivations, incentives, or techniques, promise the best success? And what feedback will ensure that the changes do pay off?"

Bureaucratic

The bureaucrat tries to ordain the future by swathing it in red tape. When people don't do what he expects, he claims it isn't his fault, because his forecasts are never wrong; nor does *he* ever fail. He says things went wrong because others didn't follow the rules. He can prove it by referring to the Policy Manual, Chapter XXX, Section MNO, page 82, paragraph IV!

Rules and standard procedures are valuable as guides and as memory aids. It's easier to turn to a page than to try to remember thousands of details. But rules summarize *past* experience. Their projection to future applications must be done with caution, with intelligence, and with humility.

Technocratic

The technocrat is the result of an autocrat or a bureaucrat "going modern" or "scientific" ("let's do it by computers"). A technocrat may also be a person who hopes to avoid human problems by hiding himself behind impersonal "scientific" procedures.

The technocrat believes: "Decisions about people are difficult and subject to error, so let's avoid them (both the decisions and the people!) by having the machines make the decisions even when they can't wholly replace the people."

Yes, machines can do a lot—much more in fact than most people dream they can—but to use the machines intelligently is one thing, to abdicate to them is another. Similarly, scientific procedures, like bureaucratic procedures, are means to facilitate the handling of masses of data and of repetitive operations. Like the rules of arithmetic and logic, they can substitute for a lot of mental sweat, but they do not of themselves forecast, much less plan and decide, what people can do, ought to do, and will do.

Autistic

The autistic person substitutes his dream-wishes for reality. He is the wishful thinker who, because he hopes something will happen, ends by believing it will happen. He wants the business to grow; therefore, it will grow. He would like to hire Tom Jones as a salesman; therefore, Tom Jones is a good salesman.

Clues to these attitudes

Following are some typical signs of the presence of the foregoing undesirable attitudes:

ATTITUDE	TYPICAL STATEMENT
Autocratic	"If these people do what I tell them to, we'll be successful. . . ." "Get results or heads will roll. . . ." "Get on the ball, or. . . ."
Bureaucratic	"If you will follow the policies exactly as set forth in the manual, you can't fail. . . ." "Don't look at me, I did my part according to the rules. . . ."
Technocratic	"As soon as we can get things under control with some flow-charts, diagrams, and data-processing systems, we'll be able to provide some decision models that will eliminate these human variables. . . ."
Autistic	"If only . . . if only . . . if only. . . ."

Creative Feedback

Chapter 6 described the Decision-Programing Cycle (DPC) in terms of the three spokes of a wheel: observation, analysis, and estimate. Chapter 7 discussed the occasions when one should delay decisions about people. Chapter 8 suggested ways of putting one's subconscious intuition and conscious energy to better use. These chapters, as well as the earlier and later ones, emphasized the importance of feedback.

To many people, feedback is equated with cold, impersonal cybernations—automatic controls, governors, valves, thermostats. But there can also be warm, friendly, human forms of feedback; for instance, the mother who returns to the crib to see if the baby has kicked off its blanket.

A steam-engine governor simply opens or closes the throttle, a thermostat simply turns the gas on or off to a furnace. But the executive who checks on his people and on their carrying out of his forecasts and decisions must do more than just "ease off" or "crack down"—blow hot or blow cold. He ought, Chapters 6, 7, and 8 explain, to keep his and their humanness in mind while he analyzes and corrects *first,* his decisions and *second,* the conduct of others.

To Understand Is Not to Invade

Chapter 9 on 3-D pictures of people; Chapter 10 on finding out facts about people; Chapter 11 on motivational patterns; Chapter 12 on people who are young, old, or creative; and Chapter 13 on patterning your approach to decisions; all obviously imply the need for much study of people. Does such study amount to an invasion of privacy? No, not if handled properly, which in essence means to analyze people for the purpose of helping them and the organization operate more effectively.

In the old days in China (and perhaps still), women would not permit male doctors to examine them. Therefore, when a woman had an ailment she would show a little statue to the doctor and point to the place on it that corresponded to the place on her own body "where it hurt." In this country we are not so shy. We expect to reveal to a doctor, lawyer, priest, or banker as much of our private lives as seems necessary. Similarly, the man who says to you, "hire me," or "promote me," must also agree to reveal enough about himself for you to know how to train, develop, and utilize him.

At first sight, it may seem paradoxical to say that the more privacy a man has, the more he risks having the wrong things known about him. But if only a little is known about a man, it is because he doesn't count; he isn't important enough to arouse people's interest! Or, if people do think about him, and they have no factual information to go on, they tend to jump to conclusions. They allow their prejudices to govern their speculations. Or they even decide, and this is a terrible judgment, that the man "is not worth thinking about."

Note the following jobs:

President of the United States   Janitor
Supreme Court Justice   Farm laborer
United States Senator   Street sweeper
Governor of a state   Clerk-typist
Military commander   Usher
Astronaut   Novelty salesman
Secret Service Agent   Parking attendant

Those in the left column are high in prestige because of their importance to society, the special education and training required, the risks involved, and the responsibilities requiring special trust and confidence. These jobs also rank high in publicity and they entail plenty of invasion of privacy. Before a military leader or a secret agent is trusted to act for the United States, his whole life is scrutinized and his personality is studied for any weaknesses. Before an astronaut enters a space ship, he has been checked out by batteries of tests. Before a man reaches high political office, the newspaper reporters and opposition "investigators" have pounced on every scrap of information about him they can find.

In short, the higher one goes, the more he lives in the spotlight. But, and this is a tremendous but, learning enough about a person to make decisions about him does not mean to gossip about him, to pry into anything not really required, or to "play God with another person's life." The guideline surely is: Look to the results the man should achieve and find out all the things, and only those things, about him relevant to his achieving the results.

Final Review

Chapter 13 and this chapter have constituted a summary of much of this book. Here, for a final, quick review are listed some of the ideas from the other chapters.

• Decisions about people are the key to all other decisions in the business. Therefore, price out each decision about a person in the four cost areas: (1) the value of his salary capitalized over the period he will be with you; (2) potential effect of any decisions, good or bad, that he can make that will affect the profit and loss statement, the condition of your assets, or the lives and fortunes of your people; (3) emotional costs of your decision to the man, to others, and to yourself; and (4) ethical costs to him, to you, and to the business.

• It's easier and cheaper in the long run to pick the right man for a job than to try to train the wrong man to do it. Good hiring practices will be the result of forcing yourself and others to review past hiring decisions. A man's success or failure is a measure not only of his abilities but of those who picked him for his assignments.

• The world is full of "facts" about people. Look into them for the answers to the questions: "What does each fact tell about this man's (1) abilities? (2) his motivations? (3) his probable future actions?"

• Hunches and intuitions are often very valuable. However, you should check under both "hot" and "cold" conditions. That is, think about a decision when you are tired and again when you are feeling dynamic. Don't allow others to force their "times of decision" onto you. Make your schedule and announce your decisions when the time is ripe for you.

• Distinguish between predictions about what a person *ought* to do and what he *will probably* do. When your executive job of predicting, deciding, and finding out failures as well as successes seems about to overwhelm you, remember that *stress* is not caused by the job, the decisions, or the other people, but by your *reactions* to such things. As a shrewd observer put it: "The thing to fear is your own thoughts about things."

● A 3-D picture of a person means a balanced view of: the past (his previous career, education, experience); the present (his job and what he thinks of it); and the future (what he hopes to achieve). Developing such a picture in depth requires probing questions and many observations, but should not involve gossip or tale-bearing.

● Commend others when they present facts about people; ignore or reprimand them when they pass along rumors, opinions, and prejudices.

● There are two viewpoints of a man: as he sees himself and as others see him. To cut past the confusions inherent in these viewpoints, use the detective's method of looking for the man's modus operandi. What has been his pattern, his customary way of behaving in various situations? From these patterns you can predict his reactions to situations in the future. You can also help him make plans to take advantage of his strengths and to offset his weaknesses.

● Finally, and most importantly, don't feel depressed over your inevitable errors in forecasting and your decisions that go wrong. From such failures comes much of the feedback which this book has praised so highly. Negative feedback from errors is not as pleasant as the positive feedback from successes, but it is just as effective a teacher!

Good luck—see Chapter 4 about luck—and good decisions about others and yourself.

Index